# LAWMEN
# CRIMEBUSTERS
# AND
# CHAMPIONS OF
# JUSTICE

**THE MEN. . .THE INSTITUTIONS
. . .THE SYSTEM AT WORK**

**John Slate and
R.U. Steinberg**

MALLARD
PRESS

An imprint of BDD Promotional Book Company, Inc.,
666 Fifth Avenue, New York, New York 10103

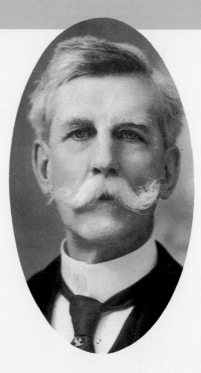

An imprint of BDD Promotional Book Company, Inc., 666 Fifth Avenue, New York, New York 10103

Copyright c. 1991 by M & M Books
First published in the United States of America in 1991 by The Mallard Press.
ISBN 0-7924-5217-8

**AN M&M BOOK**
*Lawmen, Crimebusters and Champions of Justice* was prepared and produced by M & M Books, 11 W. 19th Street, New York, New York 10011.

**Project Director & Editor** Gary Fishgall
**Editorial Assistants** Maxine Dormer, Ben D'Amprisi, Jr.; **Copyediting** Bert N. Zelman, Keith Walsh of Publishers Workshop, Inc.; **Proofreading** Shirley Vierheller.
**Designer** Delgado Design, Inc.
**Separations and Printing** Regent Publishing Services Ltd.

**Previous pages** The white-bearded Roy Bean poses with some friends outside the Jersey Lily, his saloon and courthouse.
**These pages** (clockwise from upper left) Eddie Egan, Oliver Wendell Holmes, The U.S. Supreme Court, Bat Masterson, William Jennings Bryan, and F. Lee Bailey.

# C O N T E N T S

INTRODUCTION

THE MEN

THE INSTITUTIONS

THE SYSTEM AT WORK

CREDITS

# INTRODUCTION

*Justice is truth in action.*

Benjamin Disraeli

From the dime novels of yesteryear through the shoot-em-up movies of Hollywood's golden age to the popular "true crime" best-sellers and made-for-TV movies of today, the stalwart champions of right and wrong have stood before us like supermen. And, like Superman of comic book fame, they have often come to embody "Truth, justice, and the American way." But what were they really like? Were they really *that* good?

That is one of the questions that this book seeks to answer.

Most of us know by now that much of what was written about the legendary figures of the Old West was fictional. Some stories were created out of self-serving half-truths by the men themselves; others were completely fabricated by writers seeking quick riches. Wyatt Earp, for example, was hardly the pillar of justice that he came to represent. He was a fast gun, to be sure, but he was more interested in protecting his business interests than he was in abstract concepts of right and wrong. James Butler Hickok's days as a sheriff were relatively few; drinking and gam-bling were much more important to Wild Bill. And, as for Pat Garrett, his shooting of Billy the Kid was hardly a fair fight. He simply staked out the outlaw and shot him. Maybe Bonney deserved little better, but the mode of his demise hardly made Garrett a superhero.

Still, these were the men—and their nefarious counterparts—about whom the public sought information during the early days of the information age. And it is with them

that the first part of this book, "The Men" begins. Along with the Old West's legends, you will find some more recent law enforcement officers—Eddie Egan, the "French Connection" cop, and Frank Serpico, who led a crusade against corruption in the NYPD. But, curiously, it seems that, in the modern age, those who enforce the law are less celebrated (except in fiction) than their frontier counter-parts. Instead, it is the man who defends the accused—and to some extent the man who prosecutes him or her—who get the lion's share of publicity. Accordingly, you will find a gathering of legal eagles in this chapter too, from F. Lee Bailey, the cocky Boston attorney who burst into the spotlight with his spectacu-lar second-trial defense of Sam Sheppard, the Cleveland doctor who spent ten years in prison for the murder of his wife; to William Kunstler, the flamboyant, outra-geous mouthpiece for liberal/radical causes; to Clarence Darrow, the craggy-faced, stooped- shoul-dered Chicago attorney who was the very embodiment of the word advocate. Finally, in this chapter, you will find some of the men who have interpreted the law, supreme court justices like Oliver Wendell Holmes and William O. Douglas. Their decisions keep the concepts underlying our legal system fluid and fresh.

How fluid and fresh that system is can be found in the book's third section, "The System At Work." Here landmark cases, like *Brown v. the Board of Education* and *Roe v. Wade*, illustrate how a single ruling

can fundamentally affect an entire society. Here too, cases, like the libel suit between Westbrook Pegler and Quentin Reynolds, demonstrate how private legal battles can create precedent-setting decisions, while other cases show how facets of the system beyond the courts can have their impact. In the Iran-Contra Affair, for example, we will see how the U.S. government's system of checks and balances led a watch-dog legislative branch to address abuses of power committed by the executive.

In between the sections on the men and on the system, we will look at some of the institutions that help enforce the law. These agencies—from the oldest, Scotland Yard, to the youngest, Interpol—are legendary too.

Since the origins of modern civilization, there have been those charged with the task of preserving the peace and promulgating justice. A society needs such individuals as it needs few others. Hopefully, the stories in this book and the pictures that accompany them will bring to life a few dedicated lawmen from the 19th and 20th centuries and allow you to see them in a fresh light. Hopefully, too, some of the concepts within the law will take on new meaning. As Sir William Jones, an 18th-century British jurist, wrote, "The only road to the highest stations in this country is the law." Perhaps this book will allow you to take at least a step or two on that path.

J. Edgar Hoover testifying before a senate committee in 1953. For 48 years—from 1924 until his death in 1972—Hoover was director of the FBI and one of the most powerful men in America.

The Men

# THE ONLY MAN LEFT STANDING AT THE O.K. CORRAL

## Wyatt Earp

In 1876, Wyatt Earp became the chief deputy of Dodge City, Kansas, one of the most notorious cowtowns in the West. He is shown here in the front row, second from the right, along with the town's other "peace commissioners." Bat Masterson is in the the upper row center.

*O*f all the lawmen of the Old West, none looms larger in legend than Wyatt Earp. But, like many legends, there was more to this dark-eyed, soft-spoken, and fearless gunman than the simple heroic character attributed to him by most Americans.

One of seven children, Wyatt Berry Stapp Earp was born in 1848 in Hartford, Kentucky. As a youngster, he and his siblings worked the family farm in Iowa, learning to respect the law at an early age. During the Civil War, the Earps moved to California. For the long and dangerous journey, Wyatt was given his first gun by his father. In his later years he described it as "a cumbersome weapon."

In the mid–1860s, Wyatt left home to become a buffalo hunter. By then he was a deadly shot with a six-shooter who also worked on the railroads and served as a scout for wagon trains. In 1873, Earp was in Ellsworth, Kansas, when a running battle ensued between gunslingers Ben and Billy Thompson and local lawmen. Believing the celebrated shootist to be the only man capable of bringing the Thompsons to justice, the mayor appointed Earp a deputy marshal. Wyatt justified the mayor's faith in him by successfully arresting Ben Thompson and preventing a blood bath.

The following year, Earp became deputy marshal in Wichita, Kansas. In 1876, he moved to Dodge City, where he became chief deputy. In those days, Dodge was a principal terminus for the long drives that brought cattle from Texas to the railhead. Cowboys just in from the trail were wild and raucous, and Dodge was the frequent site of brawls and gunfights. Nonetheless, Wyatt managed to restore law and order, assisted by his brother Morgan, and Bat and Jim Masterson. Occasionally, he also drew on the services of a gunslinger that he befriended in Dodge, a dentist by the name of John Henry "Doc" Holliday.

In 1879, the Earps and Doc Holliday relocated to the lively gold rush town of Tombstone, Arizona, where Wyatt was engaged as the muscle for a fancy saloon called the Oriental. Bad blood developed between the Earp contingent and a local family of dubious reputation, the Clantons, and their neighbors, the McLaurys. The ongoing feud culminated in the most famous gunfight of the Old West—the gunfight at the O.K. Corral, which took place on October 26, 1881. It lasted only 60 seconds, but when it was all over Billy Clanton and Frank and Tom McLaury lay dead, while Doc Holliday, Morgan Earp, and another of Wyatt's brothers, Virgil, were wounded. Only Wyatt was left standing.

In 1882, Earp settled in California, where his last years were spent raising horses, prospecting, serving as a boxing referee, and running a saloon. He died in 1929 in Los Angeles.

Unlike many gunfighters, Earp lived to be an old man. In 1882, he settled in California, where his last years were spent raising horses, prospecting, serving as a boxing referee, and running a saloon. He died in Los Angeles in 1929.

# THE RACKETBUSTER

## Thomas E. Dewey

In 1944, Thomas E. Dewey served as the Republican standard-bearer against three-term incumbent, Franklin D. Roosevelt. On September 7, he kicked off his campaign with this speech in Philadelphia.

*T*oday he is best remembered as the man who shocked the nation's pollsters by losing the 1948 presidential election to Harry S Truman. Before going down to ignominious defeat, however, Thomas E. Dewey had earned an impeccable reputation as a crusading district attorney, becoming perhaps the man most feared by organized crime in America.

Born in Michigan in 1902, Dewey earned a degree from Columbia Law School in only two years. He practiced privately until 1931, when he became the chief assistant federal prosecutor for the Southern District of New York. In 1935, he was appointed special prosecutor by Governor Herbert H. Lehman of New York and charged with investigating rampant organized crime throughout the state.

During his two years as special prosecutor, Dewey rounded up scores of racketeers, among them bookmakers, loan sharks, and mob leaders. His best-known case came in June 1936, when he successfully prosecuted mobster Charles "Lucky" Luciano for running a prostitution operation. Although some questioned Dewey's use of streetwalkers, pimps, and madams as witnesses at Luciano's trial, the prosecutor pragmatically said, "We can't get bishops to testify in a case involving prostitution."

A year later, in 1937, the popular crusader was elected district attorney for New York County, a powerful position that enabled him to continue pursuing big-time criminals, including Louis "Lepke" Buchalter and James Hines, an old-time politico who protected gambling in Harlem and sheltered the notorious Dutch Schultz among others. Moreover, the efficiency and organization of the DA's office became a model for the nation.

Dewey's growing reputation led him to the governorship of New York in 1942. Serving three terms as the Empire State's chief executive, he became the Republican Party's presidential candidate in 1944 but lost to Franklin D. Roosevelt. When he ran again in 1948, everyone thought he would win for sure. Instead, he became the victim of the upset of the century at the hands of Harry Truman.

By 1950, the "racketbuster" had retired from politics and settled back into private practice. He died in 1971 at the age of 69.

Special Prosecutor Dewey (right) mounts the stairs to the county courthouse in New York City for a 1935 session of the grand jury conducting a probe into racketeering. With him is one of his assistants.

# NEVER GIVE UP

## Louis Nizer

Attorney Louis Nizer, seen here in 1964, began his career as a law clerk 40 years earlier. Today, at age 89, he remains an active member of his New York legal firm.

*In his 1978 autobiography Reflections Without Mirrors, famed attorney Louis Nizer emphasized the role of perseverance in any lawyer's success. "Not to brook defeat is more than half the battle," he said. Nizer's life has been a series of victories achieved by not giving up.*

*Born in London in 1902, Nizer emigrated with his family to New York, where he grew up and attended Columbia Law School. Admitted to the New York bar in 1924, he began his legal career humbly enough—earning seven dollars a week as a law clerk. But it wasn't long before the legal community began to pay attention to the young attorney, particularly after he won his first big case, a lawsuit against the city of New York, on behalf of push-cart vendors.*

*Through his partnership with attorney Louis Phillips in 1928, Nizer became increasingly exposed to the motion picture industry. Eventually he was retained at different times to represent 20th Century–Fox, Columbia Pictures, Warner Brothers, and other major studios. In one case, he prevented movie magnate Louis B. Mayer from regaining control of Metro-Goldwyn-Mayer, the studio that he had run for decades.*

*Nizer also represented movie stars Cary Grant and Elizabeth Taylor in libel suits. In one noteworthy instance during the 1940s, he actually managed to avoid a lawsuit in a rather original fashion: while repre-senting Nobel Prize–winner Sinclair Lewis and his wife, columnist Dorothy Thompson, he learned that characters included by film director-producer-writer Otto Preminger in a screenplay were based, unfavorably, on his clients. Instead of simply going on the attack, Nizer chose instead to help Preminger rewrite the characters out of the plot.*

*In the 1950s, Nizer partici-pated in several cases in defense of individual rights. In 1954, he won the libel case of writer Quentin Reynolds against columnist Westbrook Pegler, covered elsewhere in this volume. And, in 1957, he represented radio and TV personality John Henry Faulk, who had been accused of being a Communist by AWARE, Inc., which served as the ex officio watchdog of the entertainment industry during the McCarthy era. By blacklisting Faulk for his alleged political beliefs, the organization made it virtually impossible for him to earn a living. Thanks in large measure to Nizer's brilliant defense, Faulk was awarded an unprec-edented $3.5 million in his suit against AWARE after a grueling six-year trial exposed the organization's unscrupulous tactics.*

*Today, at age 89, Nizer remains an active member of the New York firm of Phillip, Nizer, Benjamin, Krim, and Balloon.*

# NO FEET OF CLAY ON CLAY

## Clay Allison

Clay Allison was never an officer of the law. But he did bring about justice through his own sense of right and wrong and his extraordinary skill with a revolver. So great was his expertise with firearms that he earned the sobriquet "The Shootist."

Clay was truly larger than life. He was five feet nine inches tall and weighed 175 pounds, with blue eyes and dark hair, yet he seemed physically more imposing than the average 19th-century man. Even more importantly, his deeds—some true, some no doubt embellished—made him formidable indeed.

One such event was Clay's killing of a desperado in Cimmaron, New Mexico, on January 7, 1874. That day, he had been gambling with John "Chunk" Colbert, well-known in the area for a cold heart and an itchy trigger finger. Mutual distrust between the two men grew with each hand. Thus, when they sat down to dinner at the Clifton House, both men were prepared for trouble: Clay placed his pistol close at hand beside his plate; Colbert kept his weapon on his lap, cocked.

Colbert, thinking he had the drop on the famed Shootist, proceeded to raise the barrel of his weapon to table level, but

It was said of Clay Allison, known as "The Shootist", that he never killed a man who didn't need killing. He himself died in a wagon accident. (Note: this photo has not been positively identified as Allison).

Clay was too fast for him. Anticipating Chunk's draw, he ducked to the side and let the bullet sail by. At the same time, he grabbed his own pistol and put a bullet just above Chunk's right eye. Shortly thereafter, the county sheriff arrived in town to arrest Colbert for robbery, having heard that the bandit was in the area. But he discovered

that he was too late. The Shootist had dispatched the outlaw an hour earlier.

Another event that contributed to the Allison legend was Clay's fight to the death in an open grave. It seems that a man named Johnson had entered into a heated argument with Clay; soon bitter words became a challenge to a duel. It was to be a battle with a twist, however—the two wild-eyed men agreed to have a fresh grave dug, to strip, and to enter the pit. There they would fight to the death with bowie knives, the winner getting the privilege of burying the loser. Allison earned the privilege.

Clay's unglamorous death in 1887 hardly seems fitting for a man of his character. Apparently, the Shootist, who by that time had hung up his gun holster, was on a trip to purchase ranch supplies. The wagon he was driving was loaded with sacks of feed, and when one bag began to slide off, Clay tried to catch it. He slipped, fell under the heavy wagon, and one of the wheels ran over his head, fracturing his skull. On his tombstone was written, "Robert Clay Allison/ 1840–1887/He Never Killed A Man/That Did Not Need Killing."

# THE FATHER OF MODERN AMERICAN JURISPRUDENCE

## Oliver Wendell Holmes

The son of a celebrated essayist, Oliver Wendell Holmes, Jr. was admitted to the Massachusetts bar in 1867. Fifteen years later, while teaching at his alma mater, he was appointed to the state's supreme court.

He was considered one of the most progressive legal minds of his time. Teacher, scholar, and judge, Oliver Wendell Holmes, whose tenure on the U.S. Supreme Court spanned the administrations of six presidents, helped shape the American jurisprudence of today by insisting that law wasn't something set in stone but rather something to be shaped by historical circumstances.

Born in Boston in 1841, Holmes was exposed to great thinkers at an early age. His father, Oliver Wendell Holmes, Sr., was a professor of anatomy at Harvard Medical School, as well as a poet, essayist, novelist, and friend of such literary greats as Ralph Waldo Emerson, Henry Wadsworth Longfellow, James Russell Lowell, and John Greenleaf Whittier.

After receiving his undergraduate education at Harvard, Oliver joined the Union army, attaining the rank of captain during the Civil War. At the conclusion of hostilities, he attended Harvard Law School, contrary to his father's wishes, and was admitted to the Massachusetts bar in 1867. Five years later, he married Fanny Bowdich Dixwell, who was to be his wife for the next 57 years.

In 1882, while teaching at his alma mater, Holmes began his career as a judge, having been appointed by the governor of Massachusetts to the state's supreme court. During his 20 years on the Massachusetts bench, he developed a nationwide reputation for his views on labor relations. His most publicized decision came in 1896, when he dissented from his fellow justices in Vegelah v. Guntner and instead supported the right of striking furniture workers to demonstrate peacefully. This decision earned him a reputation as a radical among his peers. In Plant v. Woods in 1900, he dissented again on behalf of striking workers, arguing that to strike was "a lawful instrument in the universal struggle of life."

Seeking a progressive thinker for the U.S. Supreme Court, President Theodore Roosevelt turned to Holmes in 1902 when a vacancy occurred on the bench. Two years later, however, the friendship between the justice and the president came to an abrupt halt when Holmes failed to concur with his fellow justices over the decision to break up the railroad trust of the Northern Securities Company. In

1919, he issued perhaps his most powerful dissenting opinion. The case was Abrams v. United States, which concerned radicals found guilty of violating the Espionage Act of 1915. Even in times of war, Holmes maintained, the First Amendment guarantees every citizen the right to freedom of expression. The Great Dissenter, as Holmes came to be called, continued on the high court until 1932, when he retired at the age of 90. He died on March 8, 1935, two days before his 94th birthday.

Considered one of the most progressive legal minds of his time, Oliver Wendell Holmes was named to the U.S. Supreme Court by Theodore Roosevelt in 1902. His career as an associate justice spanned the administrations of six presidents.

# THIS GUN FOR HIRE

## Tom Horn

Tom Horn—scout, Pinkerton detective, and bounty hunter—ended his days with a noose around his neck, having been found guilty of the murder of a 14-year-old boy. He himself wove the rope that hung him.

**M**any of history's legendary crimebusters had shady sides to them. Some even started out as criminals and turned to law enforcement later on. One who went the other way was Tom Horn, army scout and Pinkerton detective, who ended his days as a blood-thirsty bounty hunter.

Born in Missouri, Tom Horn ran away from home at age 14, joined the army at age 16, and became a scout, participating in the campaign to track down Geronimo.

In 1890, after brief but successful stints as a miner and a cowboy, Horn joined the Pinkerton National Detective Agency, working out of the Denver office. Widely regarded for his relentless efficiency and for his deadly accuracy with a rifle, Horn made use of his fearsome reputation during his pursuit of a train robber named Peg Leg Watson. When Tom trailed the outlaw to a remote mountain cabin in Wyoming and announced his presence, old Peg Leg simply gave up out of fear. Neither man fired a shot!

His manhunting skills perfected, Tom quit the Pinkertons sometime around 1894, becoming instead a hired gun for the powerful ranchers who used private "stock detectives" to eliminate rustlers and pesky homesteaders. There was plenty of action for a man in his new line of work, mostly in Colorado and Wyoming, and Horn made anywhere from $300 to $600 for each cattle thief that he caught. Typically, he'd trail his prey for several days, observe his movements, and then exterminate him from a safe distance with a single shot from a high-powered rifle. Legend has it that Horn's victims were often found on the open range with stones placed beneath their heads—Tom's business card.

The restless manhunter plied his bloody trade for the rest of his life, except for a brief period in 1898 when he served as a packmaster during the Spanish-American War. His bloody misdeeds were bound to catch up with him, however, and it was his preference for long-distance rifles that finally did him in. Waiting in ambush near Cheyenne, Wyoming, for sheep rancher Kels P. Nickell on July 18, 1901, he drew a bead on the remote figure that he took to be his quarry and squeezed off an expert shot. But it was the rancher's 14-year-old son, dressed in his father's coat and hat, that Horn killed.

Everyone in Wyoming knew Horn was the murderer, but they had to prove it. Unwittingly Horn himself provided the evidence, drunkenly bragging about the Nickell incident in a Denver saloon as a deputy sheriff and a stenographer in an adjoining room took down every word. Arrested, tried, and sentenced to the gallows, the ruthless range detective calmly spent his last days writing his memoirs and weaving a fancy rope that later would hang him. Standing on the scaffolding on November 20, 1903, Tom Horn's last words were to one of the hangman's assistants: "Ain't losing your nerve, are you, Joe?"

# THE PRICE OF BEING A GOOD COP

## Frank Serpico

*It's hard to be a good cop if your fellow officers are willing to break the rules when it suits them. Still, when a good cop blows the whistle on the rule breakers, there's hell to pay. That's what Frank Serpico found out.*

*Francisco Vincent Serpico was born in 1936 and raised on the tough streets of New York City. In 1959 he became one of New York's Finest.*

*He was proud of his chosen career, but early on he discovered that there were bad cops out there—men on the take, men extorting "protection" money, and men selling confiscated drugs. When he approached his superiors about the illegal practices he encountered, his complaints went unheard. Worse, the word was out that Serpico was on a one-man crusade to clean up the department.*

*Shortly after testifying against a crooked cop who had taken thousands of dollars in bribes, Serpico was shot in the face while making an arrest. Usually cops close ranks when one of their own goes down, but in the hospital Frank received a card reading "With sincere sympathy," followed in handwriting with "that you didn't get your brains blown*

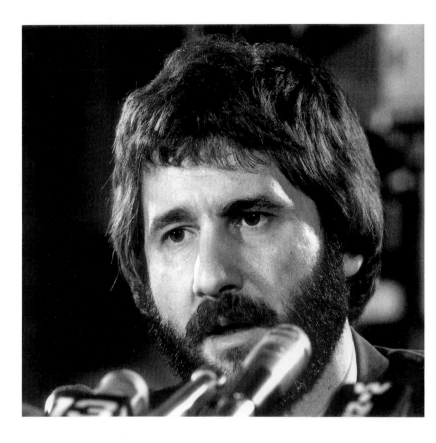

Detective Frank Serpico testifies before the Knapp Commission investigating corruption in the New York Police Department in 1971. Thanks in large measure to Serpico's crusade against bad cops, the hearings resulted in mass resignations, including that of police commissioner Howard Leary.

*out you rat bastard." Still undeterred, Serpico went to the New York Times to tell the world of the department's sordid state.*

*The resulting newspaper articles so embarrassed city officials that they finally opened an investigation into police corruption in 1971. The Knapp Commission's inquiries led to mass resignations within the department—including*

*Police Commissioner Howard Leary.*

*Still, Serpico found life in the department untenable. Finally he retired in 1974.*

*Once he was asked why he spoke out. "I did it for my sanity," he replied. The reward for his courageous deeds, he said, was his own dignity.*

# THIS TEMPLE WAS NOT SACRED

## Temple Houston

The son of Gen. Sam Houston, Temple Houston was undeniably flamboyant. He was also a passionate advocate, well-known for his courtroom oratory.

*As the youngest of Sam Houston's eight children, Temple Houston had been forced to live in the shadow of his father, the man who had been the hero of the Texas Revolution, president of the Lone Star Republic, a state senator, and a former governor of both Texas and Tennessee. But that was not a problem for Temple. He was just as flamboyant—and passionate about his work—as his dad.*

*Houston, born in 1860, was attracted to the legal profession at an early age. Graduating from college at 17 and admitted to the bar shortly thereafter, he practiced law as a district attorney in the still-untamed Texas Panhandle. After that he served as a senator in the Texas state legislature. He must have thought of his father and the revolution in which Old Sam had fought, as he initiated numerous bills to provide pensions to the children of Texas war veterans.*

*Temple was a real character who liked to sport a necktie fashioned from rattlesnake skin and to wear his hair at shoulder length, an uncommon style for the day. Outlandish though he was, Houston was also a great orator and had a firm knowledge of classical literature and history.*

*Lawyers everywhere treasure Temple Houston's "Soiled Dove" speech, his defense of Minnie Stacey, a cathouse madam who was being run out of town. When he heard of Ms. Stacey's plight, Temple, who had a soft heart for the underdog, took the case on the spot, preparing his defense in ten minutes. Invoking the biblical story of Jesus' compassion for a prostitute about to be stoned by a mob, Houston appealed to the jury's conscience, saying, "The Master, while on earth, while He spake in wrath and rebuke to the kings and rulers, never reproached one of these. One He forgave, another He acquitted. You remember both—and now looking upon this friendless outcast, if any of us can say unto her 'I am holier than thou' in the respect which she is charged with sinning, who is he?" As tears welled up in the eyes of all present, the woman was acquitted.*

# AN "UNTOUCHABLE" LAWMAN

## Elliot Ness

*F*ew lawmen in the 20th century become folk heroes. The job has simply become too reliant on teamwork, shoeleather, and patience to produce heroes in the old tradition. But one lawman of the modern age who did become a legend was Elliot Ness. As an incorruptible man in a corrupt time and place, he joined the ranks of such mythic figures as Wyatt Earp, Bat Masterson, and Wild Bill Hickok and his exploits—like theirs—became the subject of books, movies, and a classic TV series.

Ness was born in 1902 and attended the University of Chicago. At the youthful age of 26 he was chosen to head a special Prohibition squad in the Windy City, charged with the formidable task of breaking up organized crime's illegally operating breweries, distilleries, and stills. The team— handpicked by Ness—came to be known as "the Untouchables" because, in a city filled with corrupt officials, its members were thought to be above bribery.

Al Capone, the mob boss who dominated Prohibition-era Chicago, was Ness' primary target, but in actuality the Untouchables made only a minimal dent in Big Al's vast crime empire. However, they received considerable publicity for the cases they did break, thanks to Ness' insistence upon keeping the press informed about their operations.

Following Capone's arrest for income tax evasion in 1931, an investigation carried out independently of the Untouchables, Ness and his men continued their operations against Big Al's notorious successor, Frank "the Enforcer" Nitti. Later, they went after moonshine operations run by hillbillies in Kentucky, Tennessee, and Ohio.

In 1935, after the repeal of Prohibition, Ness moved to Cleveland, where he was appointed public safety director. In his new position, he cleaned up widespread corruption in the city's police department, forcing 200 resignations and sending a dozen high-ranking officers to the state prison. Ness also destroyed the operations of the Mayfield Road mob and forced gangster Moe Dalitz to move his casino operations outside of Cleveland's city limits. In addition to crimebusting, he established the city's police academy, reorganized the traffic bureau, and founded a Cleveland Boys Town.

In his later years, Ness moved to Pennsylvania with his wife and son and entered the private sector. With the help of writer Oscar Fraley, he wrote a book called The Untouchables about his exploits during Chicago's freewheeling Prohibition days. On May 16, 1957, after approving the final galleys, he collapsed suddenly and died of a heart attack.

At the age of 26, Elliot Ness became the head of a special federal squad in Chicago, charged with the task of breaking up organized crime's illegally operating breweries, distilleries, and stills. They became known as the Untouchables.

# DEAD MAN'S HAND

## Wild Bill Hickok

In 1869, James Butler Hickok was elected sheriff of Hays City, Kansas. Two years later he became marshal of Abilene, Kansas, one of the roughest cowtowns on the frontier.

**M**any Old West lawmen worked hard to develop their skills in "triggernometry" and sought astonishing escapades to enhance their reputations. Despite the abundant tall tales—many of them his own invention—one lawman who truly was fast on the draw and really did lead a raucous life went by the name of Hickok. They called him Wild Bill.

Born in Illinois in 1837, James Butler Hickok enjoyed an adventurous youth, helping his parents guide runaway slaves to freedom on the underground railroad. He left home to knock about in Kansas and Missouri, and eventually found employment as a stage-coach driver on the Santa Fe Trail. While a teamster, he met and became a lifelong friend of Buffalo Bill Cody, who would later appear with him in a stage melodrama.

How Hickok got his nick-name is subject to debate. One version has it that they started calling him Wild Bill when he served with the Union army during the Civil War in order to distinguish him from his less excitable brother Lorenzo, who was known as Tame Bill. Another account holds that one day after he stopped a lynch mob from hanging a youth, a woman was heard to say,

"Good for you, Wild Bill"—and the nickname stuck.

While the origins of Hickok's nickname may be in question, his skill as a gunfighter is beyond dispute. Of course, Bill wasn't above a little embroidery. Once he claimed to have killed a man by firing at him over his left shoulder while simultaneously outshooting another fellow in front of him; on another occasion he boasted of killing 50 Confederate soldiers with 50 bullets.

Hickok's career as a lawman was short. In 1869, he was elected sheriff of Hays City, Kansas, and two years later became marshal of Abilene, Kansas, one of the roughest cowtowns on the frontier. Then came the tragic incident in which he accidentally killed a friend whom he mistook for an opponent sneaking up on him. After that, he hung up his holster for good.

Having abandoned his career in law enforcement, Hickok traveled further west. By 1876 he had made his way to Deadwood in the Dakota Territory, where he primarily occupied himself by drinking and gambling. On August 2, he was in Saloon Number 10 playing poker. Instead of sitting in his usual seat, his back was to the door, so he was unprepared when Jack McCall, a saddletramp whom he had bested at cards, entered the saloon and shot him in the back. At the time of his death, Wild Bill was holding a full house—aces and eights—known ever since as the "Dead Man's Hand."

In addition to his career as a lawman, Hickok served in the Union army during the Civil War, was a scout for George Armstrong Custer, and even acted in a melodrama with his old friend, Buffalo Bill Cody.

# THE KING OF TORTS

## Melvin Belli

Melvin Belli, the silver-haired San Francisco attorney, is credited with having introduced the concept of "demonstrative evidence" to judicial proceedings. "Let them see and feel and even taste or smell the evidence, then you reach the jury," he maintains.

Whether he appears before a camera or before a judge, Melvin Belli displays an innate sense of showmanship. Responsible for introducing the concept of "demonstrative evidence" to judicial proceedings, this silver-haired San Francisco attorney has not only represented everyone from topless waitresses to Jack Ruby but has done some acting as well.

Born in 1907 in Sonoma, California, Belli acquired a law degree from Boalt Hall, University of California, in 1933. As a fledgling lawyer during the Depression, he found it hard to get a job with a law firm—so he signed on with the National Recovery Administration, posed as a hobo, and rode the rails across the country doing research for a migrant worker relief program. Eventually he turned to litigation, taking the case of Ernie Smith, an inmate at San Quentin Prison accused of murdering another prisoner. Belli maintained that prisons were dangerous places and that Smith had simply acted in self-defense. He won over the jury by producing a drawer from the warden's office filled with weapons that had been confiscated from the prison's inmates. This effective technique, which became known as demonstrative evidence, reflected Belli's belief that a lawyer should appeal to all the senses. "Let them see and feel and even taste or smell the evidence, then you reach the jury," he said.

In the 1950s, Belli was crowned the "King of Torts" by Life magazine for his successful suit on behalf of 79 people who had contracted polio from a defective batch of vaccine. Belli continues to welcome medically related cases. Among others, he has represented a victim of a botched sex-change operation and a girl who became permanently blind after a hospital stay.

Although he has represented many famous clients, including racketeer Mickey Cohen, comedian Lenny Bruce, and murderess Winnie Ruth Judd, he is perhaps best remembered for his defense of Jack Ruby, the man who shot and killed Lee Harvey Oswald, the suspected assassin of President John F. Kennedy, in full view of a nationwide TV audience. Belli's imaginative line of defense maintained that the Dallas nightclub owner had experienced some kind of blackout during which he shot Oswald. Although he was criticized for using this argument, which ultimately failed, Belli remains one of the country's highest paid and most respected attorneys.

Belli (left) and his co-counsel Joe Tonahill enjoyed sparring with the prosecution during the Jack Ruby murder case in 1964. In the end, however, Ruby was found guilty of the murder of Lee Harvey Oswald, the assassin of President John F. Kennedy.

# LOOSE WITH A NOOSE

## Isaac Charles Parker

For 21 years Isaac Charles Parker served as the judge for the Western District of Arkansas, a rough territory encompassing some 74,000 square miles. They called him the Hanging Judge for his swift and lethal brand of justice

**B**y the 1870s, the Indian Territory had become a haven for thieves, murderers, and others who considered themselves beyond the reach of the law. Those responsible for administering justice in the territory knew that something had to be done, but no solution presented itself. Then, a former city attorney for St. Joseph, Missouri, applied to President Ulysses S. Grant for a judgeship in the Western District of Arkansas, which included the Indian Territory, and things began to change. His name was Isaac Charles Parker.

Born in Ohio in 1838, Judge Parker was a stern Methodist and a strong supporter of Indian rights. The territory that he inherited in 1876 included nine counties in the Fort Smith vicinity, as well as the entire Indian Territory. With a total of 74,000 square miles to bring under control, the 35-year-old Parker quickly set up shop and began punishing the wicked to the fullest extent of the law. Within a few months, they were calling him the "Hanging Judge," because he had ordered the public execution of six convicted criminals en masse. After that, no one doubted that this judge meant business!

Parker held the reins of power for 21 years. During this time, he tried more than 13,000 cases, secured approximately 8,600 convictions, and sent 81 unlucky souls to the gallows.

To tackle the arduous task of rounding up fugitives, Judge Parker employed as many as 200 deputy marshals at a time; they covered hundreds of miles in some of the most dangerous territory in the country.

The judge became acquainted with many of the legendary lawbreakers of the American West, including Belle Starr, who came before him on more than one occasion for horse stealing. When another bandit, Cherokee Bill, was convicted on two counts of murder, Parker not only sentenced him to death by hanging, he also gave him a celebrated tongue-lashing, saying, "The crime you have committed is but another evidence . . . of your wicked, lawless, bloody and murderous disposition . . . another evidence of your total disregard for human life; another evidence that you revel in the destruction of human life . . . ."

During the 1890s, the Indian Territory was opened to white settlement and a more orderly way of life became the norm. With the creation of a new judicial system for the area and Supreme Court reversals starting to weigh in against him, Isaac Parker stepped down from the bench. He died shortly thereafter, on November 17, 1896.

# A POINT OF ORDER

## Joseph Welch

*Joseph Welch was an unlikley hero. In 1954, he was 63 years old and at the end of a successful but uneventful career as senior partner of a prestigious Boston law firm. Then he became counsel for the U.S. army and suddenly Welch found himself on national TV expressing the outrage that many other decent citizens felt during a very dangerous era in U.S. history.*

*During the 1950s, paranoia over Communist subversion in America created a fearful atmosphere. The ringmaster in this circus of horrors was Wisconsin's junior senator, Joseph McCarthy, chair of the Senate Committee on Government Operations. When he accused the military of harboring Communist infiltrators, the army demanded that he support his allegations. An estimated 20 million television viewers tuned in to watch on April 22, 1954, when the army–McCarthy hearings were launched.*

*As usual, "Tail Gunner Joe" was blunt and aggressive in his examination of witnesses. By contrast, Welch was calm, measured, and reasonable, continually asking the senator to support his allegations.*

*As the cross-examinations heated up, McCarthy turned his attacks toward Welch's own firm, accusing one of its junior attorneys of being a Communist. "I think I never really gauged your cruelty or your recklessness," Welch sadly replied. "Little did I dream you could be so reckless as to do an injury to that lad. . . . I fear he shall always bear a scar needlessly inflicted by you." Welch ended his off-the-cuff remarks by asking the senator if he had any decency left at all. The stinging indictment spoken so quietly hung mightily in the air. McCarthy looked like a gored bull.*

*The hearings continued for five more days, but Welch's brilliant appeal had truly marked the end of McCarthy's reign of terror. Two months later he was censured by the Senate. In 1957, his liver ravaged by alcohol, he died, a broken man. Meanwhile Welch enjoyed a degree of celebrity from the affair, hitting the lecture circuit and in 1959 portraying a judge in the film Anatomy of a Murder. He died of heart failure in 1960.*

Joseph Welch, attorney for the army during the 1954 hearings conducted by Joseph McCarthy, voiced the feelings of millions when he asked the Wisconsin senator, "Have you no decency left at all?"

# FROM SUPERSLEUTH TO SUPERSTAR

## Eddie Egan

Det. Eddie Egan of the NYPD (left) escorts French television personality Jacques Angelvin from the Kings County courthouse in 1962. It was Angelvin's limousine that served as the hiding place for the celebrated "French Connection" narcotics cache.

*He* almost became a priest and was once considered as a baseball player for the Washington Senators. Instead, he became the brains behind the breakup of one of New York City's largest narcotics rings. In more recent years, he's tried his hand at acting, producing, and writing. But no matter what line of work he's pursued, Eddie Egan has always attacked his assignments with almost fanatical zeal.

Born in the Bronx, New York, in 1929, Egan joined the New York Police Department after World War II. Chosen from among thousands of applicants, he soon came to epitomize the tough urban Irish-American cop that criminals feared the most.

It was in 1962 that Detective Egan made the bust of his career—the seizure of 120 pounds of heroin worth an estimated $32 million that had been smuggled into the United States in the limousine of a French celebrity. Author Robin Moore picked up on the story and wrote an action-filled book about it called The French Connection, *which 20th Century–Fox quickly turned*

into a blockbuster movie.

The producers were so impressed with Egan that they requested his presence on the set as a technical adviser. This in turn lead to his being cast in the movie as a respectable police lieutenant, a far cry from Gene Hackman's street-savvy "Popeye" Doyle, the character based on Egan himself.

Following his landmark drug bust, Egan spent nearly a decade on the force. Then, in 1971, after being demoted for failing to expedite the return of evidence in a drug case, he retired. What does a cop do when he's not a cop anymore? In Egan's case he goes to Hollywood to pursue a career in movies. Two additional films, Badge 373 (his old number with the NYPD) and The Seven Ups, came out of his long and outstanding career as a cop. He also made TV appearances in shows like Joe Forrester in 1975 and Eischied in 1979.

In addition to his home in southern California, Egan also kept a residence in Fort Lauderdale, Florida. His latest enterprises there have included a detective agency called Security Unlimited, whose sleuths are former U.S. marines, and a restaurant called "The Lauderdale Connection."

# BORN TO BE A LAWMAN

## Bill Tilghman, Jr.

After serving as marshal of Dodge City, Kansas, in the 1880s, Bill Tilghman moved to the Oklahoma Territory. In 1912, when this photo was taken, he was Oklahoma City's chief of police.

**B**ill Tilghman had cheated death hundreds of times. The white-haired peace officer had endured blizzards, fires, Indians, bushwhackers, and assorted deadly criminals, but was unprepared to deal with a fellow lawman, a drunken Prohibition agent whom the old man was escorting to jail. The sot, presumably disarmed, produced a hidden pistol and shot to death the legendary law enforcement officer.

It seemed that William Matthew Tilghman, Jr., was always finding himself in harm's way. Born in 1854 in Fort Dodge, Iowa, he was first exposed to danger as a weeks-old baby in the arms of his mother when an arrow from a party of attacking Sioux ripped through the sleeve of her blouse, narrowly missing him.

As a young man in the 1870s, Tilghman spent several years hunting buffalo on the Midwestern prairies. At age 23, he became a deputy sheriff under Charlie Bassett, the chief law enforcement officer of Dodge City, Kansas. In 1884, he became the raucous cowtown's marshal, establishing the innovative no-guns-in-Dodge rule that has often been credited to Wyatt Earp.

Tilghman next found action

in the Oklahoma Territory following the great Land Rush. In 1892, he was named deputy U.S. marshal by Marshal Evett Nix. Tilghman contributed more than his fair share to peacekeeping in the territory. Among others, he brought to justice "Arkansas Tom" Jones, "Bitter Creek" Newcomb, and Tulsa Jack, all members of the vicious Bill Doolin gang.

Finally, Tilghman was ready to deal with Doolin himself. Disguised as a minister, he caught up with and captured the notorious outlaw in 1895 at a health spa in Eureka Springs, Arkansas. He managed to escort the slippery Doolin back to Guthrie, the territorial capital, but the outlaw later escaped, to be killed the following year by Tilghman's colleague, Heck Thomas.

In 1900, Tilghman became sheriff of Lincoln County, Oklahoma, and 11 years later, Oklahoma City's chief of police. Toward the end of his life, with the advent of the motion picture, he got involved in the production of Westerns. In 1924, at age 70, he was persuaded to come out of retirement to clean up Cromwell, Oklahoma. As fate would have it, Tilghman, who had faced many a ruthless killer, would meet his end while attempting to disarm a drunk.

Tilghman (left) and another deputy U.S. marshal pose for a photographer in September 1893. The occasion marked the opening of Oklahoma's Cherokee Strip to white settlement.

# DEFENDING THE UNDERDOG

## Clarence Darrow

Clarence Darrow, who began practicing law in 1887, became the celebrated champion of the downtrodden and the underdog. "I am not here to defend their opinions," he once said of his clients, "I am here to defend their right to express their opinions."

Darrow appears before the House Judiciary Committee to express his strong opposition to capital punishment. In one of his most celebrated cases, he managed to help child-murderers Nathan Leopold and Richard Loeb escape the death penalty.

**W**hether or not an attorney shares his client's beliefs and opinions, it is his or her duty to fight on the accused's behalf. For championing the causes of the downtrodden and the underdog—regardless of his own feelings on the positions for which they stood—one lawyer towers above all others in legal history. His name was Clarence Darrow.

Clarence Seward Darrow was born in Kinsman, Ohio, in 1857. Admitted to the bar in 1878 and practicing from 1887 onward, this bulldog of a lawyer soon abandoned his tame, unchallenging practice for the more rigorous defense of liberal causes. One of his first big cases was that of Socialist leader Eugene V. Debs, who was accused of conspiracy. Debs, the secretary-treasurer of a railroad union, had called a strike in sympathy with another union. Violence erupted be-tween the strikers and federal troops, ending in 30 deaths. In his eloquent defense, Darrow placed Debs' predicament at the center of a larger issue— the right of unions to organize and protect the interests of their members. As a conse-quence, Debs was convicted of a lesser charge and Darrow became closely identified with the labor movement.

The crusading attorney was even better known for his spectacular criminal cases. In 1924, for example, his defense of two wealthy teenagers, Nathan Leopold and Richard Loeb, demonstrated the power of his persuasiveness. Having confessed to murdering a young boy just to see if they could execute the perfect crime, the two arrogant defen-dants were virtually certain to receive the death sentence. A long-time opponent of capital punishment, Darrow appealed to the judge's sense of human-ity and compassion to spare the two thrill killers. "Mercy is the highest attribute of men," he stressed. His protracted plea worked, and the youths were saved from the hangman's noose.

Darrow also showed bravado in 1919, when he defended members of the Communist Labor Party who were on trial for advocating the revolution-ary overthrow of the U.S. government. Enduring derision outside the Chicago court-house, Darrow inside delivered the speech of his life, a suc-cinct statement of his beliefs. "I am not here to defend their opinions," he said. "I am here to defend their right to express their opinions."

In 1938, at the terminus of an illustrious life, Darrow died at the age of 80. He was senile and nearly penniless.

# SHERIFF FOR HIRE

## Frank M. Canton

Cowboy, bank-robber, and convicted murderer, Frank Canton was twice elected sheriff of Johnson County, Wyoming. Later, as deputy U.S. marshal, he became a hired gun for the powerful Wyoming Stock Growers Association.

**O**n the broad prairies of Wyoming, wealthy ranchers were constantly threatened by rustlers. To protect themselves, they formed associations and recruited gunfighters and lawmen as private detectives. It was as one of these a range detectives that Frank M. Canton made his name.

Born Joseph Horner in Virginia in 1849, Canton and his family moved to Texas where he became a cowboy. By the time he was 26, he was wanted for bank robbery, cattle rustling, and assault; in 1874, he added murder to his list of accomplishments:.

Horner managed to flee Jacksboro, but he was caught three years later in an at-tempted bank robbery in Comanche, Texas. Escaping from jail, he turned to herding cattle, took the name Frank Canton, and eventually settled near Buffalo, Wyoming, in Johnson County.

Canton became a respected rancher under his new alias, was twice elected sheriff of Johnson County, and subsequently appointed deputy U.S. marshal. While technically he worked for the federal government, he took orders primarily from the cattle barons known as the Wyoming Stock Growers Association. This powerful group was determined to wipe out small ranchers in the area—even if it meant falsely accusing them of crimes and killing them. The feud between the cattlemen, known as the Johnson County War, lasted into the 1890s.

In time, Canton's conscience caught up with him. Haunted by nightmares and visions, he resigned his office and moved to the Oklahoma Territory, where he became undersheriff of Pawnee County and deputy U.S. marshal for "Hanging Judge" Isaac Parker.

In 1897, the restless Canton followed the gold rush to the Klondike, became a deputy U.S. marshal in Alaska, and cleaned up the lawless town of Dawson. Moving back to Oklahoma, he resumed his duties as a lawman and, in 1907, became adjutant general of the Oklahoma National Guard, a position that he held until his death in 1927.

# THE NONCONFORMIST

## William O. Douglas

*Possessing a sharp tongue, a stubborn will, and an antiestablishment outlook, William O. Douglas became almost as well-known for his independent lifestyle as he did for the keenness of his legal mind. Most of all, however, he is remembered for his passionate stands on behalf of individual rights.*

*Born in 1898 in Minnesota and raised in Washington State, William Orville Douglas grew up poor. Nonetheless, he managed to attend Whitman College and Columbia Law School, graduating second in his class in 1925.*

*Douglas' superior understanding of corporate law and economics landed him a job in a prestigious Wall Street firm. But representing corporate clients was not to his liking, so, after spending a year back home in Washington State, he joined the law faculty of his alma mater, Columbia. Douglas loved teaching, but invariably shook up the school with his fiercely independent ideas regarding business law. In 1928, he took a teaching position at Yale's Law School, where he caught the attention of President Franklin D. Roosevelt. In 1936, FDR made Douglas commissioner of the newly created Securities Exchange Commission; he became its chairman only a year later.*

*To Roosevelt, the feisty westerner well represented the creative, problem-solving spirit of the New Deal. Thus, when a vacancy became available on the U.S. Supreme Court in 1936, he nominated the former law professor. Douglas took his place on the bench easily and remained there 36 years, longer than any other justice. During that long tenure, he would often amaze—and sometimes shock—America with his opinions.*

*Among other things, Douglas warned the American public about big business, saying that "Power that controls the economy should be in the hands of . . . the people, not in the hands of an industrial oligarchy." His greatest work, however, came in civil liberties; he opposed censorship, evidenced in the pornography case Roth v. United States. He even granted a stay of execution in 1953 to convicted spies Ethel and Julius Rosenberg, which led many to call for his impeachment.*

*His spicy life off the bench kept him in the news constantly. He was married four times, each wife younger than the last. An extremely literate person, he authored more than 30 books, ranging in subject from ecological concerns to corporate law to travel adventures. Douglas suffered a paralytic stroke and retired in 1975. He died in January 1980.*

William O. Douglas became an associate justice of the Supreme Court on April 17, 1939, the date on which this photo was taken. He retired in 1975 at the age of 77, having served longer on the bench than any other justice in history.

# TOO MUCH POWER?

## J. Edgar Hoover

By 1933, when this photo was taken, 38-year-old John Edgar Hoover had built the FBI into one of the foremost crime fighting organizations in the world.

**I**t's rare that a single person can come to represent an institution, the living embodiment of an organization, but during his lifetime John Edgar Hoover was the FBI. He was also a controversial crimefighter who made as many enemies during his long administration as he did admirers.

Born in 1895 in Washington, D.C., Hoover received his bachelor of law degree from George Washington University in 1916 and his master's a year later. He began his career as a legal clerk in the U.S. Department of Justice, rising through the ranks to become head of the department's General Intelligence Division at age 24. His principal accomplishment with the division was the successful conviction and deportation of the Communist Emma Goldman. Shortly thereafter he began to work for the Federal Bureau of Investigation, becoming its director in 1924.

J. Edgar Hoover was responsible for turning the FBI into a

During the early 1960s, an aging Hoover formed uneasy relationships with President John F. Kennedy, seen here, and Attorney General Robert F. Kennedy. But he outlasted the New Frontier, serving as FBI director until his death in 1972.

polished organization of dedicated crimefighters. Among other things, the divisions of ballistics, forensics, and fingerprints were greatly improved and expanded during his administration, and promotions were made solely on the basis of merit, without regard for seniority.

During the 1930s, the director turned his attention to the problem of gangsterism, creating the celebrated list of "public enemies" to focus public awareness on criminals at large. Consequently, the likes of John Dillinger, "Baby Face" Nelson, and "Pretty Boy" Floyd became household names, as people followed the dogged investigations of these lawbreakers by the FBI.

An obsessive worker with no shortage of opinions, Hoover put his personal stamp on every aspect of bureau life. Even the margins of field reports had to be rigidly respected. "Watch the borders," the director once wrote on an agent's sloppy form. The message was taken literally, and G-men were immediately dispatched to the Mexican and Canadian borders to look for illegal activities!

During the 1940s and 1950s, Hoover continued his hunt for public enemies—then notably Communists and spies—answering to virtually no one. His not-so-hidden contempt for John and Robert Kennedy made his job difficult during the early 1960s, as he was forced to become involved in issues that he didn't favor—like the civil rights movement. However, he was on better terms with Presidents Lyndon Johnson and Richard Nixon, and was allowed to remain on the job into the 1970s, long past the mandatory retirement age. Rumor had it that his long tenure in office was due to a hidden file in which Hoover held damaging information on virtually all of Washington's power brokers.

J. Edgar Hoover died in 1972, at age 77.

# ECCENTRIC BUT EFFECTIVE

## F. Lee Bailey

Pilot, best-selling author and sometime TV talk-show host, F. Lee Bailey has probably been associated with more headline-making cases than any other attorney of the 20th century.

*He is a best-selling author and a well-known turboprop and helicopter pilot. He has even been the host of his own national TV show. But what he does best is defend people. Indeed, F. Lee Bailey has probably been associated with more headline-making cases than any other attorney of the 20th century.*

*Born in Waltham, Massachusetts, in 1933, Francis Lee Bailey received his law degree from Boston University Law School in 1960. He first came to prominence in 1964 when he secured the release of Sam Sheppard, the Cleveland doctor who was convicted of murdering his wife. Not only did Bailey get a new trial for his client, he managed to win Sheppard's acquittal in 1966. He had only been out of law school six years at the time.*

*Bailey was also triumphant in his defense of Capt. Ernest L. Medina, accused of complicity in the My Lai massacre in Vietnam, and successful in convincing the state of Massachusetts to try Albert DeSalvo, the self-confessed Boston Strangler accused of murdering 13 women, for noncapital crimes.*

*Although it seemed for a time that Bailey was infallible, he has in fact had his share of*

In 1966, Bailey (left) did virtually the impossible—he won an acquittal for Sam Sheppard, the Cleveland doctor who had been found guilty of murdering his wife 12 years earlier. Sheppard can be seen at right in this photo with his second wife Ariane.

disappointments. He lost the case of kidnap-victim-turned-radical-bankrobber Patricia Hearst, as well as one of Dr. Carl Coppolino's two murder trials. In the case of Glen W. Turner, an entrepreneur accused of illegally manipulating his businesses in a pyramid scam, the attorney was even encumbered with an indictment against himself.

Much of the controversy surrounding Bailey stems from the sometimes eccentric nature of his courtroom techniques. For example, in one appearance before the U.S. Supreme Court, when he was seeking to have a death sentence overturned, he went out of his way to get his opponent to smile amiably. His reason? "No smiling man can properly ask for another man's death," he explained. Controversial too is his use of a hypnotist as an aid in jury selections. Bailey even claims that he can tell how a prospective female juror will react to a lawyer based on the way she crosses her legs while answering questions. He has also come under attack in some quarters for his celebrity. In a profession normally noted for its conservatism, Bailey seems to enjoy the limelight.

Regardless of all the criticism leveled against him, Bailey remains a gifted, extremely well-prepared, and dedicated advocate. It is a good bet that more people in trouble would probably choose F. Lee Bailey to represent them—if they could make such a choice—over any other defense attorney in America today.

# THE LAW WEST OF THE PECOS

## Judge Roy Bean

The sign behind the bearded Roy Bean says it all. For nearly 20 years, the Kentucky-born vagabond was the Law West of the Pecos.

*H*e came to be known quite simply as "The Law West of the Pecos," a figure steeped in misty legend and Texas-size tall tales. Nevertheless, Roy Bean was a very real person who brought law and order to a wild and raucous part of Texas.

Roy was born in Kentucky around 1825. By 1848 he was roaming the West all the way to the Pacific Ocean, settling in California where he helped his brother Josh operate a saloon. During the Civil War, he appeared in San Antonio, Texas, where he began to earn a reputation as a decisive fellow.

He lived in San Antonio for about 20 years. Then, in the early 1880s, still embued with the lust for adventure, he set out to follow the railroad builders who were laying track all the way across west Texas, bringing with him a tent saloon for a livelihood. Finally, in 1882, he set up shop near the Pecos River, where the nearby town of Langtry—for actress Lily Langtry, whom Bean worshipped—would spring up. The wandering Roy Bean had at last found a home.

Although he was an honest-to-goodness judge by appointment and later by election, his brand of justice was not to be found in any lawbook. A case in point was the incident in which a dead man was brought before the judge because no one knew what else to do with the corpse. On the body they found $40 and a pistol—so Bean fined the corpse $40 for carrying a concealed weapon and confiscated the gun!

Sometimes the judge was coldhearted. When a fellow was charged with the murder of a Chinese railroad worker, Bean let the accused man go because "My law book don't say nothin' against killing a Chinaman."

Other times Roy was more benevolent. On one occasion, for example, he granted a divorce to a couple "by the law of common sense." As he put it, "I tied the knot and I have the right to untie it."

Roy was decisive alright. When he wanted something, he was not to be deterred. And in 1896 he wanted to host the heavyweight championship of the world. The problem was that the Texas Rangers would not allow the event to occur anywhere in the state. Nor would the Mexican government allow it on their side of the Rio Grande. So Bean staged the fight on a sandbar in the middle of the river between the two countries.

"The Law West of the Pecos" died in 1903.

# THE GUNSLINGER TURNED LAWMAN

## Ben Thompson

*It's hard to imagine a gunfighter becoming a lawman, but it actually happened quite often. Some towns didn't care who they hired as long as he kept the peace. One man who went from outlaw to lawman—and back again—was Ben Thompson.*

*Born on November 11, 1842, in Knottingly, England, Ben emigrated with his family to Austin, Texas, when he was nine years old. The boy had a penchant for getting into scrapes while growing up. Another penchant—one that would hasten his downfall—was gambling.*

*Like most Southern young men, Ben fought for the Confederacy during the Civil War. The end of that bitter conflict found him in the Austin city jail for the murder of another soldier. Managing to escape, he fled to Mexico where he fought for the emperor Maximilian. After a series of military defeats and the emperor's execution in 1867, Ben returned to the United States.*

*Back in Austin, he obtained the gambling concession at one of the town's better saloons and was doing quite well, but in time his temper and pugnacity earned him a two-year stay in the state penitentiary in Huntsville.*

*Following his release from prison and a subsequent trial for murder—in which Thompson was acquitted—Ben decided to run for city marshal of Austin. He lost on the first attempt but attained the office two years later. Throughout his term, Ben kept the peace, professionally and effectively, without incident. Crime dropped in the city, and it seemed that the one-time trigger-happy gunman was through with his rough and rowdy ways.*

*Then came the killing of Jack Harris. The owner and operator of the Vaudeville Variety Theater, a den of gambling, whiskey, and prostitution in San Antonio, Harris got into a dispute with Thompson over an old gambling debt and it erupted into gunplay. When the smoke cleared, the "theater" was seeking a new proprietor. Ben resigned as marshal, was tried for murder, and found not guilty. But the gambling devils were still inside of him, and he was*

*drinking more than ever. Then he and his friend John King Fisher decided to visit San Antonio again. Why, no one knows, but the two returned to the Vaudeville Variety Theater, the site of Jack Harris' death. Amid a crowd at the bar, Thompson and Fisher exchanged words with Harris' partners. An argument erupted and suddenly the two visitors found themselves alone, facing a volley of gunfire. This time Ben Thompson was the loser. The gunslinger turned marshal had been peppered with 15 bullets—nine of them in the head.*

Despite his hot temper and a penchant for gambling, Ben Thompson was elected city marshal of Austin, Texas. He kept the peace professionally and effectively until he killed a theater owner-saloon keeper in San Antonio, after which he resigned.

# ENEMY OF THE MOB

## Robert F. Kennedy

**M**illions watched on TV as the slight boyish senator with the sheepish grin thanked his supporters for their help. Following a bitter campaign against Eugene McCarthy, Robert Kennedy had won the crucial California primary. It looked as if he would, in fact, be his party's nominee for president. Within moments, however, he would be critically wounded by gun shots and the nation, still reeling from the recent assassination of Martin Luther King, Jr., would be plunged into mourning once more.

Robert Francis Kennedy was the seventh child of Wall Street tycoon and former U.S. ambassador to Great Britain Joseph P. Kennedy and his wife Rose. He attended Harvard University and received a law degree from the University of Virginia in 1951. Shortly thereafter he became an attorney in the Criminal Division of the U.S. Department of Justice, but left in 1952 to run his brother John's successful Senate campaign. During the ensuing years, Kennedy served as counsel to various federal committees, including the Senate permanent committee on investigations under Senator Joseph McCarthy. But it was as chief counsel to the Senate

In 1961, 36-year-old Robert Francis Kennedy became the youngest attorney general in U.S. history. During his administration, he took strong stands in favor of civil rights and against organized crime.

Labor Relations Committee that Bobby came into his own, attacking with a vengeance the problems of racketeering and organized crime in the nation's labor unions. In particular, he took on the powerful head of the Teamsters Union, Jimmy Hoffa. Their acrimonious hearing-room exchanges made for potent drama.

After serving as the aggressive manager of John Kennedy's successful bid for the presidency in 1960, RFK became the first cabinet member named in the new administration. As the youngest attorney general in U.S. history, he took a strong stand in the area of civil rights and continued his attacks on organized crime. He also served as a close adviser to his brother on foreign as well as domestic matters. Many credit him with effecting a peaceful solution to the Cuban missile crisis in 1962.

John F. Kennedy's assassination in 1963 brought the New Frontier to an abrupt end. A devastated Robert Kennedy remained attorney general until September 1964, when he left the administration to run for the U.S. Senate. As the junior senator from New York, he viewed himself as a "tribune of the underclass," vowing to help remedy such domestic social ills as poverty and discrimination. Other divisive issues, especially America's involvement in Vietnam, drove him to run for the presidency in 1968. He announced his candidacy for the Democratic nomination on March 16. Only three months later, on June 5, the night of his victory in the California primary, he was assassinated in Los Angeles by a lone gunman, Sirhan Sirhan.

In 1957, Kennedy (center) was chief counsel to the Senate select committee on improper practices in labor and management, chaired by John McClellan. His brother, Senator John F. Kennedy (right) was a member of the committee.

# THE MAN WHO BROUGHT DOWN "THE KID"

## Pat Garrett

*Of all the desperadoes to terrorize the Old West, none received greater notoriety than William H. Bonney, better known as Billy the Kid. Having committed his first murder in 1877 at the tender age of 17, the Kid ran rampant across the New Mexico frontier until July 1881, when he met his match in a determined lawman by the name of Pat Garrett.*

*Garrett was born in Alabama in 1850, but moved to Texas to become a cowhand and later a buffalo hunter. Six foot four in stocking feet, he made a big impression on hunters and cattlemen, particularly because of his expert horsemanship and roping skills. In 1878, he moved west to New Mexico, where he found work along the Pecos River near Fort Sumner in Lincoln County. He worked briefly as a bartender and according to legend befriended a local ranch hand named Billy Bonney, although there is little hard evidence to support the notion that Garrett and the Kid had ever been friends.*

Pat Garrett was a rancher, a bartender, a captain of the Texas Rangers and a customs collector, but he will always be remembered as the Lincoln County sheriff who killed Billy the Kid.

Called "Juan Largo" by the locals because of his height, Garrett settled in the area, married, and became Lincoln County's sheriff, promising to break up bands of rustlers who were stealing horses and cattle.

Meanwhile, in December 1880, the Kid was captured and tried for murder and condemned to the gallows the following spring—but he shot his way to freedom. Then, on the night of July 14, 1881, Garrett caught up with him on the grounds of Fort Sumner.

Spotting Billy in the doorway of a home, he fired two shots. The first one killed the Kid instantly.

Capitalizing on what was hardly a fair fight, Garrett teamed up with journalist Ashmun Upson to produce a book, An Authentic Life of Billy the Kid. Although Pat stated in his preface that the work was an attempt to clear up sensationalized accounts of the Kid's life, his book contained a number of mere legends.

Over the ensuing years, Garrett's fame continued to grow throughout the Southwest. After a brief period as a rancher, he became a captain in the Texas Rangers and was later appointed a customs collector at El Paso by President Theodore Roosevelt. In February 1908, following the financial failure of his New Mexico ranch, Garrett met a bitter end when he was shot and killed during a dispute with a feuding neighbor.

# THE MAN WHO GOT MANSON

## Vincent T. Bugliosi

Los Angeles attorney Vincent Bugliosi, seen here in a 1980 photo, gained nationwide attention during the 1970s for his innovative and impassioned prosecution of the Tate-LaBianca murderers, most notably Charles Manson.

**T**he most bizarre thing about the murders of actress Sharon Tate, coffee heiress Abigail Folger, and three others on August 9, 1969, and the slayings of Rosemary and Leno LaBianca the following day was the seeming lack of motive for the crimes. How could he get a jury to convict satanic Charles Manson and his drugged-out band of hippie followers, prosecutor Vince Bugliosi thought, if he couldn't get a jury to understand why they had acted with such callous disregard for human life?

Vincent T. Bugliosi wasn't new to complicated cases. A Minnesota native, he had graduated from the UCLA Law School in 1964 and had become an assistant district attorney for the city of Los Angeles the following year. During his eight years as a public prosecutor, he tried almost 1,000 cases, developing into a formidable advocate. But his most complicated—and celebrated—case was that of the Tate–LaBianca murders, for which he was selected out of 450 assistant DAs.

The trail from the posh homes of the LaBiancas and Sharon Tate and her husband, director Roman Polanski, led Bugliosi to a band of depraved, drug-crazed hippies called the Family living on Spahn Ranch, a former movie location in the desert. Their messianic leader, sometimes called "Jesus Christ" but better known as Charles Manson, had been identified as the mastermind of the twin bloodbaths—although he had not been a direct participant in either.

Threading through the complex issues of the case, Bugliosi eventually found what he had been seeking—a motive for the crimes. It seems that Manson believed in the inevitability of a race war that he

called "Helter Skelter," from which he and his followers would emerge as the fathers and mothers of a new society. By facilitating Armageddon through a series of random murders, he could speed up the day when his Family would inherit the earth. To be sure, Manson's theory was wacky, but it helped the jury understand why Charlie's followers had killed seven people. It also linked Manson himself to the tragic events of August 1969. Thanks to Bugliosi's ability to piece the puzzle together and to his impassioned oratory during the trial, Manson and his followers were convicted and sentenced to death (later their sentences were commuted to life imprisonment).

Vincent Bugliosi's victory earned him appointment as district attorney for Los Angeles. His account of the Manson investigation and trial, Helter Skelter: The True Story of the Manson Murders, also made him a best-selling author. In 1973, he settled into private practice, authoring several more true-crime books. He still makes his home in Los Angeles—despite death threats from Manson Family members inside and outside of prison.

# RANGER HERE, RANGER THERE

## Maj. John B. Jones

On July 19, 1878, the summer heat pounded down on Maj. John B. Jones, head of the Texas Rangers' Frontier Battalion. The major was planning to end the train- and bank-robbing spree of the notorious outlaw Sam Bass the very next day. Jones' Rangers had been tracking Bass for several months, as the bandit and his gang pulled four train robberies in the Dallas area. Then Jim Murphy, a captured member of Bass' gang, decided to switch sides, helping Jones orchestrate the ambush in exchange for his own freedom. Released to spy on Bass, Murphy was to alert Jones by telegraph of the outlaw's plans and whereabouts.

Finally, word from Murphy arrived—the Bass gang was going to hit the bank at Round Rock, a sleepy village near Austin, the state capital, on Saturday morning. Jones sent an advance party of Rangers to the town. They arrived on Friday morning to await the outlaw.

By 1878, the major had already amassed an amazing record, having served the Confederacy with distinction during the Civil War as a member of the specially organized unit known as Terry's Texas Rangers. After the war,

Maj. John B. Jones, the daring and resourceful head of the Texas Rangers' Frontier Battalion, was the man responsible for the 1878 killing of the notorious outlaw Sam Bass.

he had concentrated on the state's frontier defenses and was commissioned a major of the Frontier Battalion in 1874.

Wherever trouble surfaced, Jones was likely to be there. In 1874, for example, he helped out in the fighting at the Second Battle of Adobe Walls, a skirmish between buffalo

hunters and the Comanche chiefs Quanah Parker and Lone Wolf. Jones helped keep the peace when a dispute known as the El Paso Salt War arose in 1877 between Mexicans and Anglos over the rights to a vast salt deposit.

Then came Jones' chance to capture Bass. It was lucky that he had dispatched his men to Round Rock early, for the outlaw decided to visit the town the day before the planned robbery and plot the gang's getaway. When Jones' men spotted Bass in a feed store, they approached him. Revolvers barked, and when they turned silent Bass had been hit in the hand and the two Rangers lay bleeding. In the street, the outlaw took another hit, this time in the side, but with the assistance of one of his comrades he escaped on horseback into the nearby woods. The major found the mortally wounded outlaw the next morning and brought him back to Round Rock, where he died two days later.

Ironically, Jones didn't go out in a blaze of glory. Only three years after the Sam Bass affair, the renowned Ranger succumbed to liver disease.

# A CHAMPION OF CIVIL RIGHTS

## Thurgood Marshall

As a youngster, Thurgood Marshall was taught by his father to stand up to racial prejudice. "Son, if anyone ever calls you a nigger," Marshall senior said, "you not only got my permission to fight him—you got my orders to fight him." Thurgood learned the lesson well. As a brilliant attorney, as solicitor general of the United States, and as a U.S. Supreme Court justice, he has vigorously attacked injustice for almost 60 years.

Thurgood Marshall was born in Baltimore in 1908, the great-grandson of slaves. He attended Lincoln University in Pennsylvania and then went on to graduate first in his class at Howard University Law School in 1933. He immediately found work with the National Association for the Advancement of Colored People (NAACP), becoming the director of the organization's Legal Defense and Education Fund in 1940, a position that he held for more than 20 years.

During his tenure with the NAACP, Marshall helped lead the crusade for civil rights in many areas but especially in education. In 1950, for example, he was on the legal team that argued before the Texas State Supreme Court in Sweatt v. Painter, the case of a black man denied admission to the state university's law school. Unsuccessful on the state level, Marshall and his associates appealed to the U.S. Supreme Court, which heard the case and reversed the decision.

In 1958, Marshall, then chief counsel for the NAACP, exchanges harsh words with Dr. Virgil Blossom, superintendent of schools in Little Rock, Arkansas. The fight over school integration in the Arkansas town was among the most heated in the nation.

In 1954, Marshall returned to the high court, this time to plead in Brown v. Board of Education, reviewed elsewhere in this volume. In this landmark case, the seasoned attorney convinced the court to declare segregation unconstitutional, shattering the "separate but equal" doctrine that had dominated U.S. race relations since the 1890s.

In 1961, Marshall was appointed a federal district judge by President John F. Kennedy, and four years later was chosen by President Lyndon B. Johnson to be the country's first black solicitor general. In these positions, Marshall's major victories were again in the area of civil rights.

In August 1967, Marshall made history, when he became the U.S. Supreme Court's first African-American justice. In the intervening years, his strong stand for individual and civil liberties has been evidenced by a great many votes and opinions. But he has also continued to exhibit the independent streak for which he is famous. In 1971, for example, he dissented on an opinion that sustained New York's right to cut off a welfare recipient from benefits because she wouldn't allow inspections of her home. That year he also delivered an opinion barring draft exemptions for conscientious objectors opposed to the Vietnam War. His influence was also felt in the celebrated Roe v. Wade, which affirmed a woman's right to an abortion, and the Bakke case regarding reverse discrimination.

# HE AMBUSHED BONNIE AND CLYDE

## Frank Hamer

The Texas Rangers are well known for the lengths to which they go to get their men. Frank Hamer was no exception. From his earliest days chasing bandits along Texas' southern border to the time when he went clear out of his jurisdiction to stop the killing spree of Bonnie and Clyde, he was a model of determination.

Francis Augustus Hamer was Ranger material almost from the beginning. As a 21-year-old cowboy in west Texas, young Frank displayed uncanny man-tracking skills when he captured a horse thief on a local ranch. Impressed with his work, friends recommended that he join the state's celebrated police force, and in short order the lawman was working along the Rio Grande, keeping bandits, bootleggers, and smugglers in check.

After two years with the Rangers, Frank resigned to take the thankless job of marshaling the rough, tough town of Navasota, Texas. The political bigwigs of the town informed him that they considered themselves above the law, but that didn't stop Frank. Handcuffing one rowdy city

official who had created a disturbance, he reassured the crooked politicos. "I understand you don't allow your kind to be arrested," he said, as he led his prisoner away

After another stint patrolling the border with the Rangers, Frank was asked to help restore order to the lawless communities that had mushroomed along with the Texas oil industry. In Mexia and Borger, two particularly rough boomtowns in the 1920s, Captain Hamer had ample opportunity to demonstrate his quick and efficient methods for keeping the peace.

By 1934, Frank was retired from active duty, but a call from the state governor brought him back into service. A new crime wave was menacing the countryside, thanks to a bloodthirsty group known as the Barrow gang. Clyde Barrow, his sweetheart Bonnie Parker, and Clyde's brother Buck were the nucleus of the nefarious group that had eluded capture for two years. Like a bloodhound, Captain Hamer was on the trail.

With a determination that led him to chase the Barrow

Over the years, the no-nonsense Frank Hamer served several stints as a Texas Ranger, rising to the rank of captain.

gang far outside his Texas jurisdiction—through Oklahoma, Missouri, and Louisiana—Frank at last tracked the elusive Bonnie and Clyde to their hideout. There, near Gibbsland, Louisiana, on May 23, 1934, the celebrated bank robbers were ambushed in a blaze of gunfire as they drove down a lonely stretch of road. Hamer may have outstepped his boundaries, but he managed to get his man—and woman.

In 1934, Hamer came out of retirement at the request of the Texas governor to stop the notorious pair seen here, Bonnie Parker and Clyde Barrow. The dogged ex-Ranger tracked the bank robbers all the way to Louisiana where he supervised their ambush on May 23, 1934.

# BULLETS DIDN'T KILL HIM— FAME DID

## Melvin Purvis

In 1934, the year this photo was taken, FBI agent Melvin Purvis became an instant nationwide hero when he brought an end to the career of Public Enemy No. 1, John Dillinger.

It seems that when a lawman becomes famous, the notoriety can sometimes be more damaging than helpful to his career. A case in point is FBI agent Melvin Purvis, who rose from relative obscurity to become the heralded killer of John Dillinger, then fell back into the shadows after he was ostracized by his fellow agents and forced to quit his job.

Born in 1903, Melvin Purvis was a South Carolina attorney when he joined the U.S. Department of Justice in 1927. He began as a field agent for the Federal Bureau of Investigation, earning promotion in time to the Chicago office.

The FBI's greatest concern in 1934 was the Indiana bank robber John Dillinger, who was repeatedly eluding authorities and making a mockery of law enforcement. When the bandit pulled off a stunning escape from jail in Crown Point, Indiana, the FBI named him Public Enemy Number One— and appointed Purvis to collar him.

After following a seemingly endless trail of fruitless leads, Purvis got his break when he made contact with a Chicago madam facing deportation. Her name was Anna Sage, and she was Dillinger's lover's roommate. In exchange for Purvis' help with the immigration authorities, Sage agreed to direct the G-men to Dillinger when she, John, and her girlfriend went to the movies. That's exactly what happened at Chicago's Biograph Theater on June 22, 1934. Sage wore a red dress to identify herself to Purvis and company, who were waiting at the ready. The trio was spotted, Purvis shouted "Halt!" and when the desperado failed to stop, the agents let him have it, guns blazing.

The resulting headlines made Melvin Purvis a national hero. But the fame died quickly. A cocky attitude and what was viewed as inappropriate behavior for a G-man forced him to resign from the FBI. Thereafter, Purvis went to Hollywood, serving first as a technical adviser on gangster films and later as an announcer for the kiddie radio program "Junior G-Man." Meanwhile Purvis' former boss, J. Edgar Hoover, was busy discrediting him, trying to give responsibility for the Dillinger ambush to another agent.

In 1960, having seen his reputation besmirched and disappointed by the direction his life had taken, Melvin Purvis committed suicide. In the opinion of many, he was wrongfully denied the fame he deserved.

A month after the Dillinger killing, Purvis received the congratulations of FBI Director J. Edgar Hoover. Years later, after Purvis had resigned from the bureau, Hoover sought to credit another agent with the bank robber's slaying.

# THE WHIZ KID

## Roy Cohn

Although Roy Cohn spent more than 30 years as a practicing attorney, he will always be remembered as the wunderkind who served as Joseph McCarthy's right-hand man during the senator's investigations of alleged Communists in the government during the 1950s.

*By the time he died in 1986, he had provided legal counsel to Donald Trump, Andy Warhol, Aristotle Onassis, Mafia boss Carmine Galante, and even J. Edgar Hoover. But most people* still thought of Roy Cohn in only one way—as the aggressive anti-Communist witch-hunter who had served as chief counsel for Joseph McCarthy's Senate Subcommittee on Un-American Activities during the 1950s.

Born in 1927, Roy Marcus Cohn was exposed at an early age to the legal profession and to politics through his father, who had served on the New York Supreme Court. When he was 10 years old, Cohn even met and talked politics with President Franklin D. Roosevelt, the consummate politician of his age.

Cohn whizzed through his education, graduating from Columbia Law School at age 20. Shortly thereafter, he became a federal prosecutor, participating in several famous trials, including the notorious espionage trial of Julius and Ethel Rosenberg in 1951.

In 1952, Cohn joined Senator Joe McCarthy's crusade against American Communists and their sympathizers. Unlike his boss, Cohn had a solid working knowledge of the Communist movement in America, and he used it to help the senator root out those in high positions who were allegedly threats to American security and the American way of life. When McCarthy and Cohn decided to take on the U.S. military in 1954, however, their crusade—televised before a national audience—was seen for the witch hunt it was and it came to a screeching halt.

During the army–McCarthy hearings, a bitter rivalry developed between Cohn and a young Justice Department attorney and one-time McCarthy staffer named Robert Kennedy. This feud continued to haunt Cohn into the 1960s, when the Justice Department, under the control of then–U.S. Attorney General Kennedy, tried unsuccessfully on several occasions to have Cohn disbarred or brought up on charges stemming from his alleged links to organized crime and his rumored ethics violations.

While the army hearings destroyed McCarthy's reputation, neither they nor his feud with Kennedy stopped Cohn. Instead, he managed to develop a very successful private practice during the ensuing decades, taking on cases for well-known figures throughout the 1970s and early 1980s. In August 1986, he passed away from cardiopulmonary arrest brought on by AIDS.

# TOUGH AS A HICKORY NUT

## Charles Angelo Siringo

**D**espite the myths, punching cattle was hard work. Few men who could shoot a gun like Charlie Siringo chose to labor as a cowboy. Fewer still chose to hang up their holsters when they were still in their prime—or pick them up again when a new profession beckoned. But then the man once described as "tough as a hickory nut" had always gone his own way.

Born in 1855 to immigrant parents in Matagorda County, Texas, Charles Angelo Siringo was something of a child prodigy—by age 11, he was earning $2.50 a head for cowpunching and horse-breaking. In the 1870s, he quickly gained a reputation not only as an expert cowboy but also as a master gunslinger. His membership in the select fraternity of "shootists" brought him into contact with two of the Old West's most legendary characters—Billy the Kid, whom he befriended, and Bat Masterson, with whom he engaged in an 1877 barroom brawl in Dodge City, Kansas.

As he neared his 30th birthday, Siringo decided to give up the wild, rootless life of a cowboy and instead become a grocer in Caldwell, Kansas. He liked to recall the adventures of his youth, however, and his autobiography, A Texas Cowboy, became one of the most celebrated books written about the frontier during the 19th century.

During a visit to Chicago, he was told by a blind phrenologist who "read" the shape of his skull that he was destined to become a great detective. And, as it happened, Siringo joined the famous Pinkerton Detective Agency shortly thereafter. For the next 23 years, he pursued outlaws like the legendary Butch Cassidy and the Wild Bunch and Harvey (Kid Curry) Logan. Many of his investigations, including his capture of Efie Ladunsky, a member of the Hole in the Wall gang, involved dangerous undercover work.

After the turn of the century, Siringo retired for good, writing about his adventures as a detective and exposing the sometimes unscrupulous tactics of the Pinkertons. His point of view didn't exactly endear him to his former employers who obtained a court order to prevent him from discussing the agency in print. Although Siringo continued publishing veiled stories about the Pinkertons, it wasn't until 1915, in defiance of a court order, that he independently published Two Evil Isms: Pinkertonism and Anarchism, in which he revealed some of the capers with which he had been involved at the agency. But his success was fleeting, and Siringo died a pauper in Hollywood in 1928.

Starting out as a cowboy, Charles Siringo made his mark as a Pinkerton detective. For 23 years he served with the agency, four of which were spent tracking Butch Cassidy and the Wild Bunch.

# A CHANGE OF HEART

## William Kunstler

Since 1961, when he helped defend Freedom Riders in Mississippi, attorney William Kunstler has been known as a champion of liberal causes. In this 1985 photo, he is accusing the government of persecuting Puerto Rican nationalists, one of whom—his client—was accused of engineering a robbery.

*He* was like thousands of lawyers around the country, engaged in a safe and unchallenging practice in civil law with his brother. If anything distinguished William Kunstler, it was the books that he wrote about famous trials and courageous lawyers. He probably never imagined that one day he would be an attorney that others would write about. But then, in 1961, the American Civil Liberties Union asked him to help defend the Freedom Riders in Mississippi during the civil rights movement, and William Kunstler's life changed dramatically.

Kunstler was born in New York in 1919, majored in French at Yale, and served in the military during World War II. Following his work with the ACLU, he became more deeply involved with the civil rights movement, serving as counsel to such groups as the Student Nonviolent Coordinating Committee, and finally becoming special trial counsel to the Rev. Martin Luther King, Jr. In 1967, he led the fight on behalf of Harlem's controversial congressman Adam Clayton Powell, who was censured by the House of Representatives for improprieties.

During the late 1960s, Kunstler also became involved

with the movement protesting America's involvement in Vietnam, defending Father Daniel Berrigan and others accused of destroying Selective Service records. But Kunstler's finest hour was yet to come. In 1969/70, the trial of the Chicago Seven, covered elsewhere in this volume, turned a Chicago courtroom into street theater, as the intrepid defense attorney and his militant radical clients made a mockery of the conspiracy charges against them. Each day of the trial—or so it seemed—the presiding judge, Julius Hoffman, and Kunstler found themselves in a game of bait and retort. In one instance, Kunstler even told Hoffman that the judge made him "feel ashamed to be an American lawyer." For this and other outbursts, he received 24 citations of contempt. But five months later, Kunstler emerged victorious: his clients were acquitted of the charges against them and he became even more celebrated for his championship of liberal causes.

In the intervening years, Kunstler has continued to take on controversial cases and defend liberal causes, often at great personal expense. In 1976, for example, he defended activist H. Rap Brown from a charge of attempted murder; he has represented mafia boss John Gotti several times; and twice he successfully defended Larry Davis, the accused drug-dealer killer. One of Kunstler's more recent cases again involves the defense of seven people—this time the issue centers around the right to burn the American flag under the First Amendment to the Constitution.

# THE MASTER OF DODGE CITY

## Bat Masterson

In 1877, Bat Masterson became a member of the Dodge City police force and was later elected county sheriff. During his term of office, he became known for his ability to *talk* troublemakers into leaving town.

*T*he smoky Manhattan saloon was abuzz with activity as the young, rough customers crowded the bar to sate their thirsts. But the din of conversation suddenly faded as a stocky gray-haired gentleman entered the establishment and found a seat. The watering hole returned to its noisy atmosphere only after the man had left, for even as a senior citizen, Bat Masterson's reputation continued to precede him.

Born in 1853 in a small town in Quebec, William Barclay Masterson was one of seven children, three of whom would become lawmen at various times in rowdy Dodge City, Kansas. Having worked most of his life on farms and the open prairie, Masterson moved to the raucous cowtown in 1877 to open a saloon.

Shortly after his arrival in Dodge, he ran afoul of the town's marshal. After that, he decided never to be on the wrong side of the law again. Later that year, he joined his brother Ed on the Dodge City police force. Proving himself to be a formidable law enforcement officer, he was elected county sheriff.

During his tenure as sheriff, Masterson earned a reputation not for his skill as a gunman but for his ability to talk troublemakers into leaving town. Still, fast draws dared not challenge him because his friends John "Doc" Holliday and the Earp brothers were more than capable of avenging his death.

In 1878, Dodge turned sour for the Mastersons. First Ed was killed by gunman Jack Wagner, and then Bat failed to win reelection. So Masterson left Kansas, heading for Tombstone, Arizona, where the Earps and Holliday had set up shop. A few years later, however, he returned to Dodge albeit briefly, for a spectacular gunfight to protect his brother James, who had become city marshal.

Thereafter, Masterson traveled to Fort Worth, New Mexico, and later to Colorado, where he became a gambler. He also served as marshal in the towns of Trinidad and Creede. Later still, he opened a saloon in Denver and, in 1891, got married. Discovering a flair for writing, he landed a job in New York as the chief sports reporter for the Morning Telegram.

In 1905, President Theodore Roosevelt asked him to put on his gunbelt once again to become U.S. marshal of the Oklahoma Territory, but Bat declined. On October 25, 1921, while working at the newspaper, he died of a heart attack.

In his later years, Masterson became a sports reporter for the New York *Morning Telegram*. On October 25, 1921, he died of a heart attack while working at his desk.

# LAWFUL SLAUGHTER

## Texas John Slaughter

John Horton Slaughter became sheriff of Cochise County, Arizona, in 1887, primarily to protect his ranching interests, which were vast. He also came to own a slaughterhouse and several meat markets. This photo was probably taken around 1915 when Texas John was in his 70s.

**H**e started out as a trail boss during the days of the great cattle drives and might not have become a lawman at all if he hadn't had so much investment at stake. Texas John Slaughter was handy with a six-shooter, but his chief concern was keeping the peace so that he could tend to his extensive ranching business.

John Horton Slaughter was born in Louisiana in 1841 but grew up in Texas, where his family raised cattle. During the Civil War, he fought Indians for the Texas Rangers and later started ranching in Atascosa and Frio counties.

Despite his early successes, Slaughter decided to move on to Arizona and in 1884 bought the immense 65,000-acre San Bernardino grant, which became one of the largest ranching enterprises of its day. But there was lawlessness in the area, and Slaughter aimed to clean it up.

Even before he became a sheriff, Texas John was a threat to criminals at large. One of his future deputies, Billy King, liked to tell the story of how he and several other people were held up by a cowboy-turned-bandit named Pegleg in 1886. The word quickly spread that the desperado was headed for Mexico by way of the Slaughter ranch. A posse mounted and raced to the site, but when it got there Pegleg was already dead, with a gaping hole in his head. Slaughter said that he had located the bandit, knew he wouldn't surrender without a fight, and hadn't wanted to risk his escape—so he'd blasted him with a shotgun.

Elected sheriff of Cochise County, Arizona, in 1887, Texas John pinpointed the rowdy town of Tombstone as the area's trouble spot. He made a point of introducing himself to the local lawbreakers and quietly asking them to leave town. If they didn't, he said, they'd be dead. He always put it as simply as that. Most of the rowdies knew Slaughter's reputation for making good on his threats and cleared out. The rest he dispatched with the most businesslike of approaches—no words, no posturing, just some well-placed bullets.

In 1890, Texas John Slaughter returned full-time to his ranching enterprise and made quite a fortune. In addition to raising cattle, he owned and operated a slaughterhouse in Los Angeles and meat markets in Charleston, South Carolina, and Bisbee, Arizona. He died at the age of 80 in 1922.

Two Scotland Yard detectives—who look like they just stepped out of Central Casting—peruse the bureau's extensive fingerprint files in an effort to identify a suspect.

# THE FEDERAL BUREAU OF INVESTIGATION

Bureau agents brought George "Machine Gun" Kelly to justice in 1933. The mobster, in turn, gave the agents their well-known nickname—"G-men."

In the 1930s, the G-man was seen as an intrepid crime-fighter, doggedly pursuing tommy gun-toting mobsters like John Dillinger. In the post-Vietnam, post-Watergate era he came to be viewed as a superconservative, unimaginative bureaucrat. But even today, when people are in trouble, they are likely to yell, "Call the FBI!"

During the 19th century, the U.S. government had no specially designated crime-fighting bureau. Instead, it relied on entities such as the Treasury Department and the Department of Justice to conduct investigations in instances where federal crimes had been committed. That changed in 1908 when, at the encouragement of President Theodore Roosevelt, Attorney General Charles J. Bonaparte created a permanent force, the Bureau of Investigation (its name became the Federal Bureau of Investigation in the 1930s by act of Congress.)

During its early years, the bureau delved into the prevention of white slavery, espionage, sabotage, and draft violations. It also helped enforce such federal laws as the Mann Act of 1910, which was intended to reduce prostitution, and the 1919 Dyer Act, which prohibited the transportation of stolen vehicles across state lines. And, during World War I, it was used to round up enemy agents on domestic soil.

By the 1920s, the bureau had fallen victim to the ills that sometimes plague civil service

Early on, the bureau became known for its use of forensics, ballistics, and other facets of scientific criminology. Here, a fingerprint expert tries to define the outstanding characteristics of a set of prints.

organizations. Promotions were based on seniority, not merit, and investigations were lackluster. The organization needed shaping up, and that's what it got in 1924 when the newly appointed director, J. Edgar Hoover, undertook a thorough housecleaning, establishing rigid rules of conduct and procedure for all agents and investigations, and instituting a promotion system based solely on merit. He also turned the FBI Academy into a model of law enforcement training.

During the 1930s, Hoover led the FBI in the pursuit of gangsters like Dutch Schultz and John Dillinger. Millions of Americans avidly followed these agents' exploits in the newspapers as a way of forgetting their own troubles during the Depression. Legend has it that in one such investigation in 1933 George "Machine Gun" Kelly was cornered by officers of the bureau. "Don't shoot, G-men," he is reported to have said, thus giving the agents their well-known nickname.

In 1924, 29-year-old John Edgar Hoover became the bureau's director and for the next 48 years—until his death in 1972—Hoover virtually *was* the FBI.

# MISSING CALL FBI

THE FBI IS SEEKING INFORMATION CONCERNING THE DISAPPEARANCE AT PHILADELPHIA, MISSISSIPPI, OF THESE THREE INDIVIDUALS ON JUNE 21, 1964. EXTENSIVE INVESTIGATION IS BEING CONDUCTED TO LOCATE GOODMAN, CHANEY, AND SCHWERNER, WHO ARE DESCRIBED AS FOLLOWS:

| ANDREW GOODMAN | JAMES EARL CHANEY | MICHAEL HENRY SCHWERNER |
| --- | --- | --- |

| | | | |
| --- | --- | --- | --- |
| RACE: | White | Negro | White |
| SEX: | Male | Male | Male |
| DOB: | November 23, 1943 | May 30, 1943 | November 6, 1939 |
| POB: | New York City | Meridian, Mississippi | New York City |
| AGE: | 20 years | 21 years | 24 years |
| HEIGHT: | 5'10" | 5'7" | 5'9" to 5'10" |
| WEIGHT: | 150 pounds | 135 to 140 pounds | 170 to 180 pounds |
| HAIR: | Dark brown; wavy | Black | Brown |
| EYES: | Brown | Brown | Light blue |
| TEETH: | | Good: none missing | |
| SCARS AND MARKS: | | 1 inch cut scar 2 inches above left ear. | Pock mark center of forehead, slight scar on bridge of nose, appendectomy scar, broken leg scar. |

**SHOULD YOU HAVE OR IN THE FUTURE RECEIVE ANY INFORMATION CONCERNING THE WHEREABOUTS OF THESE INDIVIDUALS, YOU ARE REQUESTED TO NOTIFY ME OR THE NEAREST OFFICE OF THE FBI. TELEPHONE NUMBER IS LISTED BELOW.**

DIRECTOR
FEDERAL BUREAU OF INVESTIGATION
UNITED STATES DEPARTMENT OF JUSTICE
WASHINGTON, D. C. 20535
TELEPHONE, NATIONAL 8-7117

June 29, 1964

During the 1960s, the FBI became involved in cases arising from the civil rights movement. Among them was the 1964 murder of three young civil rights workers in Mississippi. This case later inspired the controversial film *Mississippi Burning*.

World War II saw the bureau assume intelligence-gathering capabilities as it investigated domestic cases of espionage and sabotage. In 1950 it began promulgating its list of "Ten Most Wanted Fugitives," and in the 1960s it helped enforce civil rights legislation and, later in the decade, pursued radical underground political groups like the Students for a Democratic Society (SDS). Perhaps the low point in the bureau's history came in the 1970s when it was used as part of the Watergate cover-up, a crime for which then-Director L. Patrick Gray was indicted (although his case was later dismissed).

The modern bureau is organized into three main sections: Law Enforcement Services, Investigations, and Administration. The first oversees the 200 million fingerprints on file, the National Academy, and the Laboratory Division, which in turn has specialized areas such as firearms, chemistry, and documents/cryptanalysis. The second section directs investigative activities on "domestic," "general," and "special" levels. The third section is responsible for published reports on crime. It also operates a nationwide teleprocessing network regarding wanted persons, missing children, and stolen articles.

The modern age has forced the FBI to confront new types of criminals and criminal activities. Here a 1984 hostage rescue team drills at the bureau's training academy in Quantico, Virginia.

Among the bureau's most celebrated—and controversial—investigations was Abscam, in which agents posing as Arabs snared 31 public officials, including a U.S. senator and several congressmen, for taking bribes.

In 1974, the FBI moved into its new headquarters, a building named for J. Edgar Hoover.

The colorful John Coffee Hays raised a regiment of 500 Rangers which fought alongside the U.S. army during the Mexican War.

Among the Rangers' most celebrated figures was Capt. Leander H. McNelly of the Special Force.

This 1878 photograph by N.C. Ragsdale shows a group of Rangers under the command of Capt. D. W. Roberts enjoying a meal on the trail.

*The early days of Anglo-American colonization on the Texas frontier saw a growing need for law enforcement. But the area's vastness and violence-prone inhabitants required peacekeepers with greater mobility than local police officers could provide and men who could combat extreme situations with virtually paramilitary strength. The law enforcement group that rose to meet these demands became legendary— the Texas Rangers.*

*The concept of a frontier defense force arose in 1823, when the "Father of Texas," Stephen F. Austin, hired ten men to act as "rangers." Twelve years later, during the Texas Revolution, this force was formally organized. Between the threat from Mexico on the Lone Star Republic's* southwest boundary and Indian raids to the west and northwest, the Rangers were not lacking for work.

The force, in true Texas style, boasted a number of colorful figures, including William A. A. "Bigfoot" Wallace, John Coffee Hays, and Ben McCulloch. Hays in particular played an important role in the Rangers' growing reputation. He was among the first, for example, to successfully employ a newly developed weapon, one that would become almost synonymous with the Old West—the Colt revolver. He also raised a regiment of 500 Rangers who distinguished themselves in battle alongside the U.S. army during the Mexican War.

Ranger activities slackened but did not cease in the era prior to and during the Civil War. But the unit gathered momentum in the Reconstruction years, and once again proved its worth in the often chaotic and lawless decades that marked the end of the 19th century. Such legendary figures as Maj. John B. Jones of the Rangers' famed Frontier Battalion and Capt. Leander H. McNelly of the Special Force helped turn the tide in many an Indian attack. They also successfully dealt with Mexican border hostilities, stage and train robberies, regional feuds, and cattle and horse thievery.

The 20th century saw a number of changes in the mode and manner of the Texas Rangers. With membership on

The old ways, embodied by Stetsons, boots, six-shooters, and horses meet the technology of the modern age—walkie-talkies and helicopters.

The Rangers' famed Frontier Battalion stood as Texas' first line of defense in border hostilities with Mexico. It also helped prevent stage and train robberies, regional feuds, and cattle and horse thievery.

*the decline, the institution was reorganized and modernized in 1935 and placed under the direction of the Texas Department of Public Safety, which continues to administer Ranger activities today. Despite the changes, however, the Rangers have continued to successfully meet the challenges posed by societal disorder—as witnessed by their successful ambush of Bonnie and Clyde during the 1930s and their efforts at riot control during the Texas oil boom. As an old-time Ranger put it, "No man in the wrong can stand up against a man in the right who keeps on a-comin." And that's what the Rangers do.*

In this photo circa 1989, a Ranger administers a polygraph test to a young suspect.

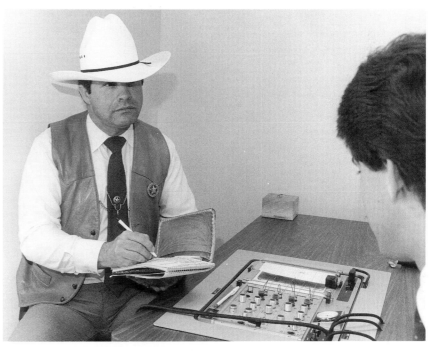

# THE SÛRETÉ-NATIONALE

It is hard to imagine a time when law enforcement agencies didn't use fingerprinting, rogues' galleries, and undercover surveillance to solve crimes, but these practices are not really that old. They were pioneered by the respected French crimefighting institution the Sûreté-Nationale, and their development can be traced to the legendary, 19th-century ex-convict-turned-detective, Eugène-François Vidocq.

Vidocq was a master thief with an encyclopedic knowledge of crime and criminal methods. In 1809, when Paris was experiencing a major crime wave, he approached the municipal authorities about the prospect of organizing a group of plainclothes agents who could help infiltrate the underworld. With the grudging approval of the administration, he handpicked a force of 20 ex-cons, all with specialized skills, and greatly reduced the crime rate. It was Vidocq's "security brigade" that became known as the Sûreté.

A number of Vidocq's procedures have become part and parcel of police work. Undercover surveillance, for example, originated when Vidocq had his people pose as common criminals so that they would be imprisoned and thus learn from other inmates about crimes, proposed and actual.

Elaborate disguises for field work were also employed.

Vidocq treated sleuthing as a science and turned the Sûreté into an incredible resource for information on criminal activity. Detailed records were kept on suspected individuals, and rogues' galleries—initially in the form of sketches and later by means of photos—were utilized for identification. Interrogation techniques were also developed to draw out inadvertent confessions from suspects.

Among the Sûreté's most celebrated cases was its hunt

Eugène-François Vidocq was a master thief with an encyclopedic knowledge of crime and criminal methods. The unit of 20 ex-convicts that he turned into a crime-fighting force in 1809 became known as the Sûreté.

Part of Vidocq's legacy to the Sûreté was its extensive resource material on criminal activity. Detailed records were kept on suspected individuals, and rogues' galleries—sketches initially and later photos—were used to identify perpetrators.

Perhaps the Sûreté's finest moment came in 1921 with the capture of this man, Henri Désiré Landru, the notorious "Bluebeard of Paris" who had seduced, robbed, and murdered at least ten women.

in 1912/13 for the Bonnot gang, bank robbers who used the newly invented automobile to make their getaways thanks to the gang's leader, racecar driver Jules Joseph Bonnot. After a 15-month pursuit, the crimefighters finally cornered Bonnot and his gang and ended their crime spree after a six-hour gun battle.

But perhaps the Sûreté's most famous case occurred in the 1920s. At the time Paris was plagued by a man the newspapers called "Bluebeard." A clever con man, he preyed on lonely women, seducing them, inducing them to sign over their money and possessions to him for "safe-keeping," and then disappearing. In time, he began to take not only their valuables but their lives as well. Finally, in 1921, the Sûreté's commissioner, Jean Belin, discovered the identity of this con-man killer—an accountant named Henri Désiré Landru, whose notebook contained a list of Bluebeard's victims. Thanks to the Sûreté's sleuthing, Landru was tried, convicted, and guillotined.

Today the Sûreté-Nationale has four major subdivisions: Counter-Espionage, the Criminal Investigation Division, the Special Branch (which oversees airports, railways, and seaports), and Public Security. Like the FBI, its American counterpart, it has offices located throughout the nation that operate in conjunction with local authorities.

# THE PINKERTON DETECTIVE AGENCY

Allan Pinkerton, the Scottish-born founder of the Pinkerton National Detective Agency, had tried his hand at barrel making and local politics, among other things, before establishing a private police force in Chicago.

During the Civil War, Pinkerton and his operatives, shown here with Abraham Lincoln (at right edge of tent), tracked down Confederate spies and gathered intelligence for the Union.

The wide-open eye in the company's logo says it all, for vigilance and determination have always characterized the Pinkertons, the oldest privately owned detective agency in the world. While the organization is no longer actively involved in the apprehension of criminals, its rich tradition links it to some of the most colorful—and troubled—periods in American history.

The origins of the Pinkerton National Detective Agency can be traced to the controversial career of its founder, Allan Pinkerton. Born in Scotland in 1819, he arrived in the United States in the early 1840s and involved himself in a number of endeavors—barrel making, local politics, even maintaining a successful way station on the Underground Railroad—before becoming a crimebuster. In 1844, he gained an early reputation in the field when he went undercover to help break up a Chicago counterfeiting operation, an "adventure" that perhaps inspired him to make a career of detection and security. At any rate he eventually established a private police force to patrol the dangerous streets of Chicago.

As Pinkerton's services grew in demand, the agency branched out, offering protection and surveillance throughout the West for the burgeoning railroad industry. In 1860, the firm was hired to protect a most important railway passenger—President-elect Abraham Lincoln—on his journey from Springfield, Illinois, to the nation's capital. After Pinkerton foiled an assassination plot against Lincoln before he even assumed office, the new chief executive hired the master detective and his company to track down Confederate spies and gather intelligence for the Union during the Civil War. One of Pinkerton's great triumphs came in 1863, with his successful exposure of the Washington spy ring headed by the cunning Southern belle Rose Greenhow.

In the 1870s the Pinkertons pursued a plethora of bank and train robbers, including the notorious Jesse James. James—who had killed two Pinkertons—was holed up with his family at a farmhouse in Clay County, Missouri, in January 1875, when the "Pinks" laid plans for a raid. Jesse had gotten wind of the plot, however, and was long gone by the time the detectives arrived. During the ensuing melee, Jesse's half-brother, a mere eight-year-old, was killed and the outlaw's mother seriously wounded. Jesse James swore vengeance on Allan Pinkerton, who deeply regretted the incident.

Meanwhile, the Pinkerton Agency continued to flourish. The 1880s and 1890s saw the outfit ally itself with big business, as it protected railroad and coal mining companies against the growing organized labor movement during a period marked by

One of Allan Pinkerton's greatest triumphs came in 1863, with his successful exposure of the Washington spy ring headed by Rose Greenhow, seen here with her daughter.

heated strikes and bloody confrontations. After the turn of the century the agency pared down its activities. Today it provides security services for a wide range of fields and its investigation services include undercover assignments, the investigation of insurance claims, and consumer attitude testing.

Allan Pinkerton's oldest son William became a member of his father's intelligence-gathering force during the Civil War. He was 17 at the time. Later, he took charge of the Chicago office and, upon his father's death in 1884, inherited the family business, which he ran with his brother Robert.

The wide-open eye in the company's logo and the motto "We never sleep" are testaments to the vigilance and determination that characterized the world's oldest private detective agency.

The "bobbies" of today are nicknamed for Home Secretary Sir Robert Peel, who in 1829 led the fight in Parliament for a well organized, professionally trained metropolitan London police force.

# SCOTLAND YARD

In its early days, the London Metropolitan Police Force made its home at Whitehall Palace in the Great Scotland Yard, hence the organization's nickname. The site had once held the palace of a medieval Scottish nobleman.

They all wear tweeds, smoke pipes, and carry magnifying glasses. Physically they are not imposing, but they are dogged in their use of scientific methodology to track down criminals in cases that on the surface appear to offer no clues. That is how most people think of Scotland Yard's detectives. And indeed in little more than a century, this world-renowned organization—officially known as the London Metropolitan Police Force—has raised crimefighting to an art.

Scotland Yard traces its origins to the 18th and early 19th centuries, when the streets of London were patrolled by an untrained group of policemen called the Bow Street Runners after the location of their headquarters. As the Industrial Age changed the nature of urban life, this force proved ineffective in checking crime. In 1829, the problem became so great that it drew the attention of Home Secretary Sir Robert Peel, who led the fight in Parliament for a tightly organized, professionally trained unit of 3,000 men. They

Bobbies engage in a gas mask drill during World War II. In addition to their regular duties, they assisted the air raid and Civil Defense wardens during the Battle of Britain.

At the heart of Scotland Yard's international renown is the Criminal Investigation Division (CID) which helped pioneer a scientific approach to criminology, developing extensive files on criminals, a forensic laboratory, and the use of fingerprinting and photography.

became known then as "peelers," and today they're called "bobbies." Either way, the nickname serves as a reminder of Peel's dedication to law and order.

The new police force made its home at Whitehall Palace in the Great Scotland Yard, hence the organization's nickname. The site had once held the palace of a medieval Scottish nobleman. A new building was constructed in 1890 abutting on the Thames River. This in turn was replaced by New Scotland Yard in 1967, located near Victoria Station.

During the first years of its existence, Scotland Yard operated like most other urban police organizations of its day. Then, in 1878, it forged a new chapter in criminology when it created the Criminal Investigation Division (CID). This special branch helped to pioneer a scientific approach to crimefighting, developing extensive files on criminals, a forensic laboratory, a fraud squad, and the use of fingerprinting and photography. Mobility was enhanced through horsedrawn carriages, replaced later by cars equipped with two-way radios. To train specialists,

*a detective school was insti-*
*tuted.*

*The history of Scotland Yard is rich with celebrated cases cracked by the force's detectives. One of the most vivid is that of Dr. Hawley Harvey Crippen, who in 1910 poisoned his wife, dismembered her, and sealed the corpse under the brick floor of his basement. Crippen and his lover Ethel Le Neve then disguised themselves—Le Neve as a boy—and booked passage on a steamer out of the country. Noticing Crippen and Le Neve's departure, Chief Inspector Walter Dew of Scotland Yard engaged in a thorough search of the doctor's home, pulled out a loose brick in the basement, and made the grisly discovery. The lovers were caught, and Crippen was tried and hanged.*

*Scotland Yard today fights new strains of crime. Because of the Irish Republican Army, for example, it is extensively engaged in activities designed to combat terrorism and bombings. It is also responsible for protecting government officials and visiting dignitaries and, as the agency that registers the nation's vehicles, it is deeply*

A modern skyscraper became the headquarters for the Metropolitan Police Force in March 1967. Located near Victoria Station, it was nonetheless called New Scotland Yard in deference to the organization's celebrated nickname.

In recent years, the Metropolitan Police have had to learn to combat new forms of crime. Here bobbies undergo public order training, necessary for coping with riots.

*involved in incidents concerning cars. Finally, the institution coordinates the operations of all British law enforcement agencies with the activities of Interpol, the International Criminal Police Organization.*

Patrolling the Thames has been part of Scotland Yard's duties since 1838, when the Marine Police Office became part of the London Metropolitan Police Force. Motor boats were introduced in 1910.

Today's bobby – as much a symbol of London as the Tower or Buckingham Palace.

# INTERPOL

During the 20th century, the rise of mass communications and the great advances in technology around the world brought criminal activity to a global level. Moreover, new types of international crime—like money laundering, terrorism, and art theft—emerged. Clearly, the law enforcement community had to develop a response to the changing conditions. It came in the form of a multinational crimefighting entity called the International Criminal Police Organization, or Interpol.

Interpol was largely the brainchild of Dr. Johann Schober, head of the Vienna police and a former chancellor of Austria. Dr. Schober felt that by cooperating, the police forces of nations around the world could become more effective at deterring crime within their borders and catching offenders as the crimes occurred. With these goals in mind, he sponsored a world conference of law enforcement officers in Vienna in September 1923. The resulting organization would grow dramatically over the years to meet the ever-increasing rise of transnational crime.

Initially Interpol was headquartered in Vienna. When Nazi Germany annexed Austria in 1938, the institution became defunct. But it was resurrected in 1946 at a conference in

After World War II, a resurrected Interpol relocated from Austria to France. This photo shows the office of Jean Nepote, who was the organization's secretary general from 1963 to 1978.

In 1970, when this photo was taken, Interpol was headquartered in St. Cloud near Paris. The organization officially moved to Lyons in 1989.

Brussels, Belgium. Since then the central offices have been located in France, first in Paris and more recently in Lyons.

Interpol does not make arrests or participate in the physical apprehension of criminals. Instead, it gathers and provides information to over 100 member countries to facilitate the investigations of their own police forces. The millions of files, including fingerprints and mugshots, are housed at Interpol's Lyons headquarters.

Usually the organization prefers to maintain a low profile, but Interpol made headlines in the 1980s when it played a major role in exposing a money-laundering and drug-trafficking scheme known as the Pizza connection. Two Mafia families,

Interpol gathers and provides information to the police forces of more than 100 member countries. Its millions of files, including fingerprints and mugshots, are housed at the organization's headquarters, seen here in a photo taken in 1968.

it was discovered, were smuggling heroin into the United States—but no one could determine how the drugs were being distributed or how the profits were being laundered. Careful work by Interpol traced the heroin from Turkey to Sicily to America, where money was being filtered through Mafia-owned Italian restaurants and pizzerias. Interpol also followed the convoluted trail of bank accounts established by the mob in several countries, and this sealed the fate of those involved. It all ended in 17 convictions and $2.5 million in fines.

Each year delegates attend a meeting of the Interpol General Assembly, hosted by member countries on a rotating basis. The meeting seen here, held in the United States in 1985, saw the election of the organization's current secretary general, Raymond Kendall of Great Britain.

The president of Interpol from 1984 to 1989 was an American, John Simpson (right), also chief of the U.S. Secret Service. He is seen here with the French Interior Minister Charles Pasqua prior to an Interpol meeting in 1987.

Testifying before the Senate Watergate Committee in June 1973, former White House counsel John W. Dean III dispassionately revealed the illegal activities and gross abuses of power conducted by the executive branch of the government.

The System At Work

# A MONKEY'S UNCLE

## Tennessee v. John Thomas Scopes

To prosecute the case, the state brought in William Jennings Bryan, three-time Democratic party candidate for president and a die-hard religious fundamentalist.

**A**re man and woman divine creations or, as Charles Darwin would have it, did they descend from the apes? In Tennessee in the 1920s, the answer was clear—Tennessee sided with God. Consequently, it was against the law to teach Darwin's theory of evolution in the state's school system. Was the law right? That's what two of the foremost figures of the day set out to debate.

John T. Scopes, a 24-year-old high school science teacher in Dayton, Tennessee, decided to test the validity of the prohibition against teaching evolution. When he introduced the subject in his curriculum he was arrested. To prosecute the case, the state brought in a heavy hitter—William Jennings Bryan, three-time Democratic party candidate for president and a die-hard religious funda-mentalist. To defend Scopes came that celebrated champion of liberal causes, Clarence Darrow.

The trial of Tennessee v. John Thomas Scopes opened on a sweltering summer day, July 10, 1925, in the Dayton courthouse. Bryan treated the event like a tent revival meet-

ing, using quote after quote from the scriptures to back up his argument that God's law was supreme and those who thought otherwise were devoid of Christian morals.

Clarence Darrow's approach was different. Gripping his suspenders as he paced the floor, he sought to prove that the law against teaching evolution was illegal, for it violated fundamental rights guaranteed in the Constitution. The highlight of the battle came when Darrow forced the old-fashioned orator to admit on the witness stand that he did not believe in the literal truth of the Bible—using the six days of creation as the trap. No, Bryan confessed, he didn't think the world had been created in so short a span. If the length of time that it took to create the heavens and the earth could be subject to interpretation, Darrow's argument went, so too could the means by which humankind

was created.

Darrow won the argument—but the jury still found John Scopes guilty. After all, he had never denied violating a state law. For his "crime," the teacher was fined $100.

Bryan was broken by the trial, which made him an object of ridicule even to his supporters. He died of apoplexy on July 26, only five days after the proceedings ended.

Ironically it was later revealed that Scopes never actually violated the law for which he was tried. The teacher had missed a class session during the school year, the session that was to include the discussion of evolution!

The defendant, school teacher John T. Scopes (center), and other members of the Dayton community gathered around a table in Robinson's Drug Store to show photographers how their discussions on evolution ultimately gave rise to the "Monkey trial."

In July 1925, people from all over came to the little community of Dayton, Tennessee, to witness the titanic battle between Darrow and Bryan. It was part trial, part circus, and part revival meeting.

# A SOLDIER'S DUTY?

## The Court-Martial of Lieutenant Calley

Lt. William Calley, Jr., leaves the courthouse at Fort Benning, Georgia, on April 1, 1971, having just been given life imprisonment for his role in the My Lai massacre. The sentence was subsequently commuted to 20 years.

**W**as he ordered to kill innocent Vietnamese civilians or did he act on his own? Either way, Lt. William Calley became known as the officer in command at the bloody My Lai massacre and his military trial attracted worldwide attention as he faced charges of war atrocities, one of the few American soldiers ever to be so accused.

In the disastrous Vietnamese conflict, much of which was fought in the farmlands and villages of South Vietnam, distinctions between those supporting the Viet Cong and those who were innocent civilians were often difficult to make. Those who guessed wrong, often on the basis of appearances alone, sometimes left innocent people dead. That's what happened on March 16, 1968, when Lt. William Calley, a 24-year-old 1967 enlistee, entered the village of My Lai with his platoon and ordered his men to indiscriminately kill nearly every person in the place, including women, children, and the elderly. Some reports placed the death toll as low as 22; others claimed up to 347 victims. A year and a half after the massacre, Calley was brought to trial for his actions.

During his court-martial, the lieutenant denied responsibility for the massacre, claiming that he had been ordered to carry out the slaughter, but his superiors denied having issued any such orders. It came down to a case of his word against theirs, and it

Paroled in 1975, Calley returned to his hometown, Columbus, Georgia, where he married Penny Vick in June 1976. He has since become a salesman in his father-in-law's jewelry store.

wasn't Calley that the tribunal chose to believe. Even though 25 people were implicated in the massacre, all were acquitted except him.

The conviction was handed down on March 21, 1971, and Calley was sentenced to life imprisonment. The intervention of President Richard Nixon saw the sentence reduced from hard labor to house arrest. Later the term of imprisonment was reduced from life to 20 years. Meanwhile, a battery of lawyers continued the fight on Calley's behalf, and through a writ of habeas corpus the lieutenant was released on bond in early 1974. Later that year Calley's conviction was overturned because, in the opinion of the court, he had not received a fair trial. It was indeed a moment of jubilation for the young man, but it wasn't to last. Almost a year later, the original verdict was reinstated on appeal.

Paroled in 1975, Calley nonetheless continued in his efforts to clear his name. In 1976, he played his last card, appealing to the U.S. Supreme Court, but the justices declined to hear the case. Upon his release from incarceration, Calley returned to his home in Columbus, Georgia, where he became a salesman in his father-in-law's jewelry store.

# EQUAL EDUCATION FOR ALL

## Brown v. Board of Education

The United States has always prided itself on being a "land of opportunity," but throughout its history it has given more opportunities to some than to others. Although amendments to the U.S. Constitution following the Civil War seemingly opened up a new world of freedom to African-Americans, the civil rights movement of the 1950s was still struggling to ensure that those rights would indeed be granted.

During the period of Reconstruction, newly freed African-Americans saw a brief period of political and social power in the South, as the defeated Confederacy was occupied by the U.S. army and former rebel soldiers were precluded from holding office. But in the 1880s and 1890s, as white control reasserted itself through poll taxes, literacy tests, and intimidation by the likes of the Ku Klux Klan, blacks became second-class citizens. In 1896, in the landmark case of Plessy v. Ferguson, the U.S. Supreme Court mandated that separate facilities along racial lines were acceptable, as long as the facilities were equal. Thus, segregation became the law of the land and signs above drinking fountains and bathrooms marked "For Coloreds Only" and "For Whites Only" became common. In public schools, separate facilities were also maintained, but they were hardly equal. According to one estimate in 1930, every seven dollars spent to educate a white child in the South was matched by only two dollars for a black child.

"In the field of public education, the doctrine of 'separate but equal' has no place," wrote Chief Justice Earl Warren in *Brown v. the Board of Education.* "Separate educational facilities are inherently unequal." He is seen here addressing the membership of the American Law Institute a few days before the decision was handed down.

The attorneys who argued on behalf of the plaintiffs were (left to right) George E.C. Hayes, Thurgood Marshall, and James Nabrit, Jr.

'separate but equal' has no place. Separate educational facilities are inherently unequal."

It was a landmark decision, but to enforce it required years of struggle, as little children marched into formerly segregated schools in the company of policemen and National Guardsmen, often to be vilified by hostile whites. Still, the case was a major step toward the realization of a truly multiracial society—a struggle that is yet to be fully resolved.

Finally, in the early 1950s, things began to change. It started when Linda Brown, an 11-year-old in Topeka, Kansas, decided that she didn't want to attend a school a great distance from her home when there was one just five blocks away. She sued the Board of Education, which insisted she attend the distant African-American school, and lost. In its decision, the court maintained that "the buildings, transportation, curricula, and educational qualifications of the teachers" at the black school were substantially equal to those provided to white students and thus in conformance with Plessy v. Ferguson.

Then the U.S. Supreme Court decided to hear the case and those of several other African-American children around the country who had been forced to attend segregated schools.

The plaintiffs were represented by attorney Thurgood Marshall and backed by testimony supplied by the NAACP. It took two years for the Supreme Court to hear all of the testimony, but after six months of closed-door decision making, it announced its ruling on May 17, 1954: in a unanimous vote, it decided in favor of the plaintiffs. Writing for the court, Chief Justice Earl Warren stated, "In the field of public education, the doctrine of

This photo serves as a poignant reminder of the young people affected by the decision to integrate public schools more than 50 years after segregation became the law of the land in Plessy v. Ferguson.

# WRITE OR WRONG

## The Reynolds–Pegler Libel Suit

The plaintiff—war correspondent and columnist Quentin Reynolds.

The defendant—Pulitzer Prize-winning columnist Westbrook Pegler.

*T*he 1940s found newspaper columnists Westbrook Pegler and Quentin Reynolds at the pinnacle of their respective careers. Representing opposite ends of the political spectrum, they were both well aware of the power of the printed word—and often wielded that power in their columns. But one day one of them went too far, touching off a landmark court case between the two that set the tone for libel suits for years to come.

The case began simply enough in 1949 when Quentin Reynolds was assigned by the New York Herald Tribune to review a biography of the noted newspaperman and union activist Heywood Broun. Authored by Dale Kramer, the book's final passage detailed Broun's last days, during which he was severely troubled by attacks in print from anti-Communist columnist Westbrook Pegler. Reynolds chose to mention this portion of the book in his review.

Pegler, incensed by the book review, which he saw as a form of character assassination, retaliated by telling the readers of his widely syndicated column that Reynolds had been a World War II profiteer, had faked his stories as a war correspondent, and was a notorious coward. He also accused Reynolds of proposing marriage to Broun's widow while accompanying her to her husband's funeral, and of collaborating with Broun to arrange for the seduction of "a susceptible young white girl" by "a conspicuous Negro Communist."

In Reynold's opinion, Pegler's verbal attack had gone beyond the bounds of fair comment and criticism, leading him to consult with the famous trial lawyer Louis Nizer about a possible lawsuit. Nizer told him he had formal grounds to claim libel, but warned that such charges would be extremely difficult to prove. Not only would they have to show that Pegler had written untruths about Reynolds, they would also have to prove that he had done so maliciously and that the allegations had damaged Reynolds' reputation. In short, Nizer warned, they faced a long, potentially expensive legal battle with the possibility of nothing at the end to show for their trouble. Willing to proceed anyway, Reynolds filed charges against Pegler in 1949, seeking $50,000 in damages.

The high point of the trial came when Nizer squared off against witness Pegler, getting the pompous columnist to admit that what was supposed to have been a quote in his column from someone who knew Reynolds was in actuality the result of Pegler's own phrasemaking. Finally, in May 1954, five years after Reynolds had filed suit, the jury ruled that the column had indeed been libelous, and awarded Reynolds a record-setting $175,001. Not only was that three and a half times more than the plaintiff had asked for, it was the largest settlement ever awarded in an American libel case to that point.

The story of the case was documented in a best-selling book by Nizer and subsequently dramatized in the 1966 Broadway play A Case of Libel, later adapted for television. Ironically, Pegler sued the producers of these shows for invasion of privacy, but before any of the cases came to trial, Pegler died in the spring of 1969.

Military desertion is a very serious crime, especially during wartime, and it has a history of harsh punishment. Often the charges are leveled against people who cannot, or will not, bear arms. Such was the case of Pvt. Eddie Slovik, the only deserter during World War II to be executed—out of 40,000 known cases.

Born in Hamtramck, Michigan, in 1920, Edward Donald Slovik was as American as apple pie. Prior to entering the army, he worked in a plumbing business and later served as a drugstore clerk. He was basically a good kid, but he seemed born to lose. Twice, in 1937 and again in 1939, he committed petty larceny, ending up both times in the Michigan State Penitentiary.

On parole after his second stint in prison, young Slovik tried to make good. He got married, took a job at an automobile plant, and looked as though he had finally found the stability he needed to stay out of trouble. Then, in January 1944, he was drafted. That was the beginning of the end for Eddie Slovik.

He was miserable in the army. He wasn't soldier material and was showing it—through teary letters and discussions with fellow soldiers.

Sent to France in August 1944, with the 109th Infantry, Slovik and another private either got lost or were separated from their unit. Attaching themselves to a Canadian regiment for two months, the soldiers finally caught up with their comrades on October 8. After only a few hours back in camp, Slovik panicked and ran, but he turned himself in the next day. Although desertion charges were brought against him on October 19, he was given an option—he could go to the front or face a court-martial. He refused to fight.

The hastily arranged trial gave Slovik almost no opportunity to prepare an adequate defense. To make things worse, his advocate, Maj. Edward Woods, was neither a lawyer nor did he have any formal legal training. The private pleaded not guilty, but he was convicted of the charges. Perhaps because of his past criminal record, the tough military tribunal decided to make an example of him and sentenced him to death by firing squad. Even an urgent letter from the condemned prisoner to the Allied supreme commander Gen. Dwight D. Eisenhower was to no avail.

On January 31, 1945, Pvt. Eddie Slovik was executed in St. Marie aux Mines in the Vosges Mountains of France without the granting of even a last request. Slovik's widow was never officially informed of her husband's court-martial, just his death. It was only through a book by writer William Bradford Huie that the facts of the case finally came out. Nonetheless, the U.S. army has not recognized any miscarriage of justice rendered in this case.

# MILITARY JUSTICE

## The Execution of Private Slovik

Pvt. Eddie Slovik, the only American deserter executed during World War II. He was shot in 1945, at the age of 25, one year after this photo was taken.

# LAWBREAKING IN THE NAME OF PATRIOTISM

## The Iran–Contra Affair

Senator Daniel Inouye of Hawaii, chairman of the Iran-Contra Committee, swears in Lt. Col. Oliver North on July 7, 1987, the first day of the assistant national security adviser's testimony before the committee.

*On November 3, 1986, Al Shirra, a Beirut newspaper, reported an astonishing story—that the United States had been secretly selling arms to Iran in the hope of obtaining the release of Americans held hostage in the Middle East. Such an action seemed unthinkable, but in time America learned that the arms sale was only part of an incredible story. For a nation just barely recuperating from Watergate, the emerging revelations about lying, secrecy, and abuse of power within the executive branch of the government seemed all too familiar.*

*Nine days after the Al Shirra story broke, President Reagan admitted that he knew about the arms sale—itself a staggering confession. Later, on November 25, however, he revealed the second bombshell in the affair—that some of the money received from Iran had been given to the Contras, an anti-Communist rebel organization in Nicaragua. Giving aid to the Contras, like selling arms to Iran, was prohibited by law. That same day, two of the major parties in what became known as the Iran–Contra affair left the White House. They were the president's national security*

adviser, Adm. John M. Poindexter, and his assistant, Lt. Col. Oliver North. On November 26, the president appointed John Tower to head a three-man inquiry into the affair. Meanwhile, Congress prepared to conduct its own investigation.

The Tower Commission report came out first. Released on February 26, 1987, it laid principal blame for the affair with the president, citing as well Donald T. Regan, the White House chief of staff. Two and a half months later, on May 5, hearings conducted jointly by the House and Senate began under the chairmanship of Senator Daniel Inouye of Hawaii. Throughout the summer, a national TV audience watched the parade of 28 witnesses testify to the sordid sequence of events. The high point of the hearings—indeed the high point of the whole affair—came when Oliver North took the stand. Looking and sounding every inch a hero, the 43-year-old marine officer, testifying under limited immunity, explained for six days how he had lied to the Congress and the American people and had put patriotism above the law.

On November 18, 1987, the 690-page Congressional report was released. "The common ingredients of the Iran and

Looking and sounding every inch a hero, the 43-year-old marine officer testified for six days before the congressional investigating committee. He admitted under the promise of limited immunity that he had lied to the Congress and the American people and had put patriotism above the law.

Members of the Tower Commission, appointed by President Reagan to investigate the Iran-Contra affair, included (left to right) former secretary of state Edmund Muskie; John Tower, former senator from Texas; and Brent Scowcroft, national security advisor to President Ford.

A pensive John Poindexter, former national security advisor, explains his role in the Iran-Contra affair to the congressional committee.

Contra policies," it concluded, "were secrecy, deception, and disdain for the law." According to Chairman Inouye, the affair had exposed the existence "of a secret government within our government."

During the course of the hearings and subsequent trials, almost all of the perpetrators admitted that, in the process of carrying out their duties—which included regular appearances before congressional committees—they had misled lawmakers and had indeed perjured themselves. North, Poindexter, and several others were subsequently convicted of crimes, but their sentences were light and usually suspended. A final conclusion about Reagan's knowledge of or participation in the covert activities has never been reached.

Fawn Hall, North's former secretary, added a bit of glamour to the Iran-Contra affair. She is seen here testifying before the congressional investigating committee on June 9, 1987.

# POOR LITTLE RICH GIRL

## The Gloria Vanderbilt Custody Case

At the heart of a two-year custody battle—and one of the most publicized cases of all time— was this little girl, Gloria Vanderbilt, heiress to a $4 million estate.

On one side of the custody battle was little Gloria's mother, Mrs. Reginald Vanderbilt, the former Gloria Morgan. She is seen here in a 1925 photo with baby Gloria and her husband, a grandson of Commodore Cornelius Vanderbilt.

On the other side of the battle was Mrs. Harry Payne Whitney, the former Gertrude Vanderbilt. She is seen here leaving the courthouse during the custody hearings in 1934 with a pensive ten-year-old Gloria and a man believed to be her attorney.

*In the midst of the Great Depression, the plight of one little girl—a millionairess to be exact—touched the conscience of a nation. At the young age of ten, little Gloria Vanderbilt, an heiress to a $4 million estate, found herself in a tug-of-war between her mother and her aunt that resulted in one of the most publicized custody cases of all time.*

*Gloria, great-granddaughter of tycoon Cornelius Vanderbilt, was just a year old when her millionaire father, Reginald Claypoole Vanderbilt died suddenly. For a decade she remained in the custody of her mother, Gloria Morgan Vanderbilt. But Mrs. Vanderbilt, whose extravagant lifestyle included endless trips between New York, London, and Paris, hardly had time to play mom. As a result, little Gloria spent most of her life in the care of a nurse.*

*Mrs. Vanderbilt's sister-in-law was Gertrude Vanderbilt Whitney, a talented sculptor and patron of avant-garde art (the Whitney Museum of American Art in New York bears her name). Not exactly the model of upper-class propriety herself, Mrs. Whitney was nonetheless appalled at her niece's upbringing. To rectify the situation, she filed for custody with the New York Supreme Court in 1934 and won. Furious with the decision, Mrs. Vanderbilt brought habeas corpus proceedings to recover possession of her daughter. And the tug of war was on. Finally Gloria got her own day in court. The little girl answered the questions that were put to her in a straightforward manner, but when asked about her mother she expressed her feelings with apprehension and later broke into sobs.*

*On November 21, 1934, the decision was handed down: custody was awarded to Mrs. Whitney. In the words of the court, Mrs. Vanderbilt's upbringing of Gloria was "in every way unfit, destructive of health, and neglectful of her moral, spiritual, and mental education." By Judge John F. Carew's order, Mrs. Vanderbilt could only see her daughter on weekends, Christmas Day, and during the month of July.*

*Still the battle was far from over. During the next couple of years, as Gloria visited her mom under heavy guard by tommygun-toting detectives, Mrs. Vanderbilt tried to have the decision reversed through the appeals process. Again, little Gloria was dragged through the same traumatic litigation process to which she had been exposed before. Finally, a resolution was achieved in January 1936, when the New York Supreme Court dismissed Mrs. Vanderbilt's appeal once and for all. After that, Gloria settled into a relatively quiet life, making the news only occasionally, as when she got married. But the limelight found her once again—nearly 35 years after the custody battle—when she became one of the leaders of the designer jeans craze.*

# THE RIGHTS OF THE ACCUSED

## The Escobedo and Miranda Decisions

In *Escobedo v. Illinois* (1964), the U.S. Supreme Court ruled that this man, Danny Escobedo, had been denied the right to legal counsel before he confessed to the murder of his brother-in-law.

*Under the guidance of Chief Justice Earl Warren, the U.S. Supreme Court made a number of landmark decisions during the 1950s and 1960s, decisions that brought sweeping political and social changes to the American scene. With two rulings in particular,* Escobedo v. Illinois *in 1964 and* Miranda v. Arizona *in 1966, the Warren court significantly changed the way law enforcement personnel carried out interrogations and at the same time guaranteed certain rights to those accused of crimes.*

*The first case involved Daniel Escobedo of Chicago, who was charged with the 1960 slaying of his brother-in-law. Under police interrogation, he confessed to the crime and was convicted of murder at his trial. There had been no attorney present during Escobedo's interrogation by police. In a 5–4 decision, the Supreme Court ruled that Escobedo's confession had been obtained illegally because he had been denied his right to legal counsel during police questioning, a right guaranteed to him by the Sixth Amendment of the Constitution.*

*In the second case, Ernesto Miranda was arrested in 1963 for stealing eight dollars from a bank employee. While in custody, a young rape victim saw* him in a lineup and named him as her assailant. Although he initially refuted the accusation, after two hours of intense questioning Miranda confessed to the crime and signed a written affidavit to that effect.

In this case, the Supreme Court ruled that the police had failed to advise Miranda of his right against self-incrimination, a right guaranteed to him under the Fifth Amendment of the Constitution. Expanding upon its ruling in Escobedo v. Illinois, the court mandated a stiff code of police conduct during investigations, stating that law enforcement officers had to inform suspects of their rights and that suspects had to be allowed to seek legal representation—or to have representation provided for them—before any interrogation could begin.

During the years since the Escobedo and Miranda cases, the court rulings have come under considerable fire from law enforcement officials who claim that the decisions have placed unreasonable burdens on them. To be sure, suspects whose guilt was certain have been set free because they were improperly "Mirandized." Many legal experts believe that the procedures mandated by the court will continue to come under scrutiny and perhaps even be modified in years to come. But the fundamental rights established in these landmark cases will never be taken away.

In *Miranda v. Arizona* (1966), the U.S. Supreme Court overturned the conviction of Ernesto Miranda because he had not been properly advised of his right against self-incrimination prior to confessing to the kidnapping and rape of a young woman.

With the *Escobedo* and *Miranda* decisions, the court significantly changed the way law enforcement officers dealt with persons under arrest. From left to right, the justices who handed down the decisions were (front row) Clark, Black, Warren, Douglas, Harlan; (back row) White, Brennan, Stewart, and Fortas (replacing Goldberg who was on the bench for *Escobedo*).

# ALL-AMERICAN NIGHTMARE

## The Trial of Dr. Jeffrey MacDonald

**O**n February 17, 1970, six months after the drugged-out followers of Charles Manson perpetrated the gruesome Tate–LaBianca murders in Los Angeles, an unrelated but equally bizarre and horrifying group of homicides occurred at the home of Dr. Jeffrey MacDonald in Fayetteville, North Carolina. Found semiconscious and badly wounded, MacDonald, then a captain in the Green Berets, told police that a drug-crazed band of hippies had entered his home and killed his pregnant wife and two daughters. He recalled that one of them wore a floppy hat and a short skirt, chanting "acid is groovy, kill the pigs!"

Despite MacDonald's story, the army accused him of the killings, but dismissed all charges after a lengthy military hearing. Convinced that his son-in-law had literally gotten away with murder, Alfred Kassab brought the facts of the case to the attention of the U.S. attorney general's office, which conducted its own investigation. In 1975, an indictment for murder was returned against MacDonald.

In the meantime, the doctor had resigned from the army and moved to California. When he finally came to trial in 1979, MacDonald, who had achieved a certain level of local prominence

Green Beret captain, Dr. Jeffrey MacDonald, awaits the 1970 decision of a military tribunal investigating charges brought against him for the murder of his wife and two children. All charges were dropped.

*in his new life, continued to maintain his innocence. In support of his story about the woman in the floppy hat, the defense produced Helena Stoeckley, a schizophrenic substance abuser. Although she had told others that she had been present on the night of the murders, she claimed on the witness stand to have never entered the house or to have seen MacDonald. The prosecution countered by establishing the doctor's involvement in an extramarital affair—a possible motivation for murder—and his abuse of drugs.*

*Dr. MacDonald was convicted of second-degree murder on August 29, 1979, and sentenced to three consecutive life terms in prison. The following year, a federal appeals court reversed the conviction, contending that the doctor had been denied a speedy trial as guaranteed by the U.S. Constitution. Then, in 1982, the U.S. Supreme Court overturned the appeals court's decision and reinstated the original sentence.*

*Over the years, MacDonald's case has received considerable attention from the media. A year after the Supreme Court's ruling, author Joe McGinniss wrote a best-selling account of the story, Fatal Vision, which supported the notion of MacDonald's guilt. This, in turn, became the basis for a TV miniseries. Then, in 1989, a documentary film, False Witness, by Ted Landreth, suggested that the doctor's story may in fact have been true, a conclusion shared by a 1990 segment of the TV series 20/20.*

MacDonald's father-in-law, Alfred Kassab, refused to accept the findings of the military tribunal. His dogged pursuit of the case led to a trial in 1979, at which MacDonald was convicted. Kassab is seen here with his wife Mildred after the return of the jury's verdict.

*As of this writing, MacDonald continues to be imprisoned, but it may well be that the last of his case has yet to be heard.*

# A CASE OF ESPIONAGE

## The Trial of Julius and Ethel Rosenberg

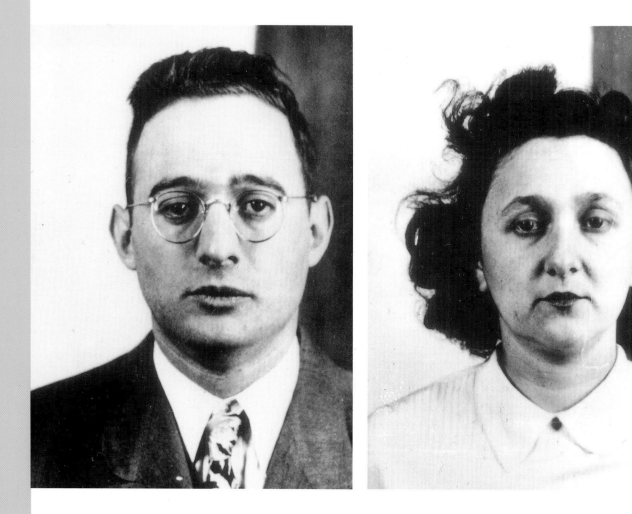

The members of the so-called A-bomb espionage ring included (far left) a New York electrical engineer, Julius Rosenberg; (left) his wife, Ethel; (right) his brother-in-law, David Greenglass, a machinist at Los Alamos; and (far right) Morton Sobell, a friend of the Rosenbergs, also from New York.

It was a time of prosperity. The war had been won. The flight to the suburbs had begun. And people were producing babies at an unprecedented rate. But the late 1940s also saw America's World War II ally, the Soviet Union, become a bitter foe. Still Americans weren't too worried, for in the Cold War—as it was called—they held the trump card: they had the A-bomb. Then, suddenly in 1950, the Soviets became a super-power, too. And America was mad as hell. The folks accused of giving Russia the key to the nuclear clubhouse were Sgt.

David Greenglass, a machinist at Los Alamos, the nation's top-secret research facility; a New York electrical engineer, Julius Rosenberg, Greenglass' brother-in-law; Julius' wife, Ethel; and Morton Sobell, a friend of the Rosenbergs, also from New York.

Now the nation had tangible targets for its sense of outrage and betrayal. Greenglass was sentenced to 15 years' imprisonment because he had confessed to the FBI and served as the chief witness against his associates. And Sobell, whose role in the affair was considered somewhat less important, was granted a separate trial, found guilty of espionage, and awarded 30 years in prison. That left the Rosenbergs.

The trial of The United States v. Julius and Ethel Rosenberg opened on March 6, 1951. Although the defendants emphatically denied any role in delivering the secrets of the A-bomb to the Soviet Union, the prosecution went to great lengths to establish their guilt, with a rough sketch of a bomb—allegedly passed by the Rosenbergs to the Russians—becoming a key document in the case. The extremely persuasive prosecutor, Irving Saypol, appealed to the jurors with a closing argument rich in lurid imagery: "Imagine a wheel. In the center of the wheel, Rosenberg, reaching out like the tentacles of an octopus . . . all the tentacles going to the one center, solely for the one object: the benefit of

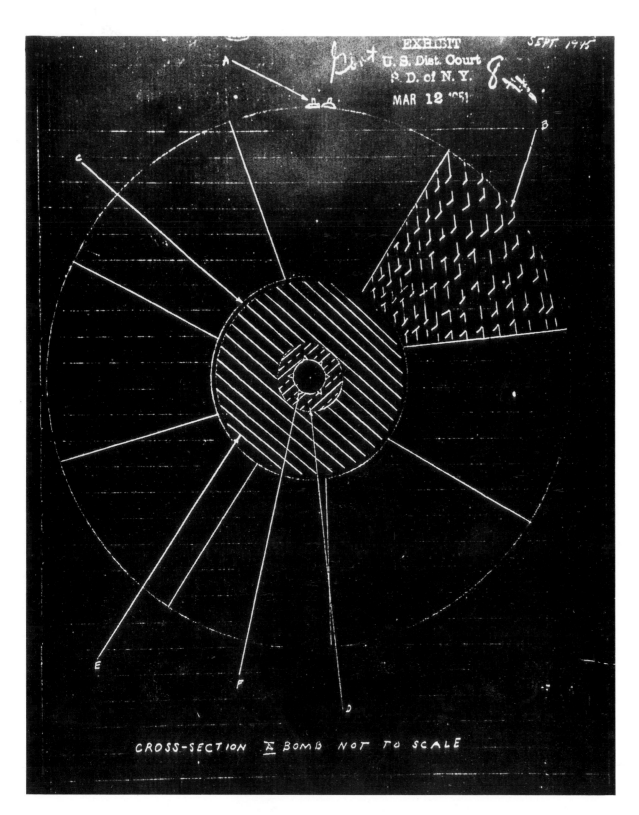

This sketch, a cross section of an A-bomb which the Rosenberg purportedly gave to the Russians, served as a principal piece of evidence against Julius and Ethel at their trial.

The sight of the Rosenberg's sons, Michael, age five, and Robert, age nine, visiting their parents at Sing Sing Prison added an element of poignancy to the pending electrocutions.

Soviet Russia." The Rosenbergs were found guilty and sentenced to death in the electric chair.

But it wasn't over. Many around the world were outraged that the mild-looking man and woman were to die, the first U.S. civilians to be executed for espionage. Two years' worth of appeals followed, accompanied by demonstrations around the globe, with many thousands demanding that the Rosenbergs' lives be spared. But to no avail. The Rosenbergs were electrocuted on June 15, 1953.

The ensuing years have seen the Rosenbergs emerge as the quintessential victims of the anti-Communist hysteria that gripped America in the early 1950s. Questions about their roles as master spies linger but—whether they were guilty or not—few would point to their trial as a model of impartial justice at work. And even many of those who do accept the Rosenbergs' guilt still wonder whether they deserved to die for their crime.

People the world over protested the death sentences handed down to Ethel and Julius Rosenberg. The demonstrators seen here were part of a group of nearly 400 picketing outside the U.S. courthouse in Chicago shortly before the executions were carried out in June 1953.

# SETTING THE RECORD STRAIGHT
# OR RUSH TO JUDGEMENT?
## The Warren Commission

On September 24, 1964, Chief Justice Earl Warren delivered to President Lyndon Johnson the report of his commission on the assassination of John F. Kennedy. Surrounding them are the other commissioners (left to right): McCloy, Rankin (counsel), Russell, Ford, Dulles, Cooper, and Boggs.

It didn't take long for the questions to start flying. Had Lee Harvey Oswald acted alone or had he been part of a conspiracy to kill President John F. Kennedy? Was Oswald killed by Jack Ruby to hush him up? To quell the rumors, the new president, Lyndon Johnson, ordered a full investigation into the events of November 22, 1963, one week after the assassination and asked Chief Justice Earl Warren to head the probe. Joining Warren were Allen W. Dulles, former head of the CIA; Hale Boggs, Democratic congressman from Louisiana; John Sherman Cooper, Republican senator from Kentucky; Richard B. Russell, Democratic senator from Georgia; John J. McCloy, a prominent lawyer and former high official; and Gerald R. Ford, Republican congressman from Michigan.

Several avenues of inquiry were to be explored, but the most important questions were, first, did Lee Harvey Oswald kill the president and, second, was the assassination the result of a conspiracy. The commissioners were determined to find the answers and to support their conclusions with hard evidence. To this end, they amassed thousands of pages of eyewitness testimony, as well as police and lab reports, assisted by the FBI, the Secret Service, and state and local authorities. The finished product, 888 pages long, was presented to President Johnson on September 24, 1964; 26 supplemental volumes of exhibits and testimony were published two months later. Within days, paperback editions of the report were available to the general public and it became an instant best-seller.

The Warren Commission concluded that indeed Lee Harvey Oswald had acted alone, killing Kennedy with three shots fired from the sixth floor of the Texas Schoolbook Depository in Dallas. It further concluded that Jack Ruby, who killed Oswald on November 24, 1963, had not been acquainted with the assassin nor had Ruby been part of a conspiracy. Finally, the commission found no evidence of a conspiracy on the part of any federal, state, or local authorities. The report also contained numerous criticisms of the Secret Service's performance before and immediately after the assassination. Its recommendations designed to safeguard future chief executives included building searches prior to presidential visits and checks on persons who are potential threats to a president's safety. There was also a call for law enforcement groups and the news media to set ethical standards for the dissemination of information regarding large-scale crimes like this one, so that the legal process would not be hindered in future investigations.

Although the report was intended to set the record straight regarding President Kennedy's assassination, rumors and theories about what actually happened persisted. There were those who believed that the commission had "rushed to judgment"—to paraphrase attorney Mark Lane, one of the report's more vocal critics. Some even accused the commissioners of being part of a massive cover-up. Even today, more than 25 years after the assassination, new evaluations of the evidence occasionally emerge. And, in a bizarre twist, Oswald's widow, Marina, recently announced her belief that her husband had been framed. Thus, it seems that, despite Earl Warren's best efforts, a general consensus about what transpired on that dark November day may never be attained.

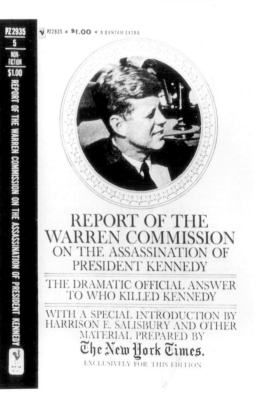

Within days of the official release of the Warren Commission report, paperback editions were in book stores and on newsstands. The "official answer to who killed Kennedy" became an instant best-seller.

# FALLING STAR

## The Acquittal of Fatty Arbuckle

**S**ometimes a trial can have implications that extend beyond its impact on the participants. It may create a cause célèbre—as in the Rosenberg case—or alter public perception. It may even lead to the passage of new laws. One case created such a furor that it changed an entire industry for decades. At its center was a portly, fun-loving man. They called him Fatty, and the industry that he changed made movies.

Born in 1887, Roscoe "Fatty" Arbuckle was an immensely popular film funnyman. In 1921, he commanded an income of $5,000 a week, which made him Hollywood's highest paid actor. Off-screen he lived a life as excessive as the "Roaring Twenties" itself, enjoying wild parties brimming with illicit booze and bustling with immodest guests. One such affair took place in the comedian's suite at the St. Francis Hote! in

San Francisco on September 5, 1921—Labor Day weekend. The all-day bacchanal peaked during the afternoon, as showgirls, film industry people, and politicians caroused about in a boozy haze. Arbuckle was after one starlet in particular, Virginia Rappe, whom he had gotten drunk and enticed into his bedroom.

Suddenly, the guests were startled by screams of pain emanating from the fat jester's room. Forcing their way in,

Rappe's girlfriends Zey Prevon and Bambina Delmont discovered a hysterical Virginia tearing at her clothes and screaming, "I'm hurt! I'm dying!" Four days later Virginia died, the victim of peritonitis (from a ruptured bladder).

Lurid stories of the actress' demise soon appeared in papers from coast-to-coast. In what had become the most shocking scandal in Hollywood's relatively young history, Fatty Arbuckle found himself pilloried, his career in ruins. Worse, the comedian faced murder charges after turning himself in to the San Francisco police the day following Rappe's death. Amid newspaper headlines howling for blood, the actor was tried— not once but three times!

The first trial began on November 18, 1921. Among the evidence presented against Arbuckle was an affidavit from the deceased's friend Bambina Delmont. Curiously, though, she never took the witness stand. The proceedings ended in a hung jury, with most of its members in favor of acquittal. The second trial brought a guilty verdict, but Arbuckle won a new trial on appeal, and this one, held in 1922, found the comedian not guilty. Fatty was off the hook, but his life was a shambles and his money blown on legal fees.

Although Arbuckle stood innocent before the law, the public never forgave him. He made a disastrous comeback bid, slipped into severe alcoholism, and died in 1933 of a heart attack. He was 46.

While Arbuckle rather quickly faded from public memory, the impact caused by his trials and the revelations of his scandalous behavior had a long-lasting effect. Faced with public outrage at the morality not only of the comedian but of the Hollywood community in general, the motion picture industry decided that it had to police itself or risk regulation from the outside. Thus was born the Hays Office, named for its chairman, former Postmaster General Will Hays. From that point until well into the 1950s the Hays Office monitored every movie that Hollywood released and anything that was seen on the screen had to be approved by its guardians, men and women who regulated the language and mores of the cinema through a rigid Production Code.

A dour Arbuckle with his attorney Frank Dominquez. Legal fees for the comedian's three trials—plus his inability to earn a living—left him in financial ruin.

The legacy of the Fatty Arbuckle case was the appointment of former postmaster general Will Hays as the studios' rigorous arbiter of morality and decency. He is shown here at the 1939 opening of *Gone With The Wind*, which was allowed to retain the word "damn" only after considerable debate.

# ABUSE OF POWER

## The Watergate Affair

Bob Woodward (left) and Carl Bernstein were the dogged reporters for the *Washington Post* who pursued the Watergate story when virtually no one else was interested in it.

**I**t began with a third-rate burglary and ended with the resignation of a U.S. president. In between, many of America's most powerful officials confessed to lies, gross abuses of power, and the commission of felonies, making the name of a hotel and office complex in Washington, D.C., synonymous with the biggest scandal in American history.

The affair began on June 17, 1972, when five men were caught attempting to bug the Watergate offices of Lawrence O'Brien, chairman of the Democratic National Committee. The event largely went unnoticed in that presidential election year, as the incumbant, Richard Nixon, seemed headed for a landslide victory. But two dogged

reporters for the Washington Post, *Carl Bernstein and Bob Woodward*, pursued the story, finding, first, that some of those involved in the break-in had connections to the Committee to Re-elect the President (CREEP) and/or the administration and, second, that a huge slush fund was being used by CREEP to finance not only the Watergate break-in but other questionable practices.

Meanwhile, the administration, under the direction of White House counsel John Dean, was engaged in a cover-up designed to ensure that investigations into the affair ended with the burglary. But rumors continued to fly, and Woodward and Bernstein kept digging. Moreover, at his sentencing, one of the burglars, James McCord, accused President Nixon of complicity in the crime and asserted that witnesses had perjured themselves during the burglars' trial.

In spring 1973, the Senate Select Committee on Presidential Campaign Activities began its inquiry into the affair under the chairmanship of Senator Sam Ervin of North Carolina. Among those who came forward to testify were John Dean, who had turned himself in to federal authorities, and presidential aide Alexander Butterfield, who revealed that tape recordings existed of the president's private meetings.

Chairman of the Senate Watergate Committee, Sam Ervin of North Carolina holds up checks received by CREEP which were allegedly used to fund the Watergate break-in. Samuel Dash, the committee's chief counsel, is at right.

Watergate grew out of the Nixon administration's "insatiable appetite for political intelligence," former White House counsel John W. Dean III told the Senate committee investigating the scandal.

With Butterfield's dramatic revelation, the investigation took on new life. Refusing to give up the tapes, Nixon finally released edited transcripts of some of them. But the demand for the tapes continued. The affair reached its boiling point on October 20, 1973, when Nixon ordered the firing of Archibald Cox, the special prosecutor for an independent Watergate investigation, because of his continual demand for the tapes. After what became known as the "Saturday night massacre," the president's position was virtually untenable. Worse, the new special prosecutor, Leon Jaworski, also demanded the tapes.

The final act of the drama came in the summer of 1974. As the House Judiciary Committee soberly considered the possibility of bringing impeachment proceedings against the president, the U.S. Supreme Court ordered Nixon to release several previously undisclosed tapes. One of them, that recorded on March 23, 1973, clearly showed the president participating in the cover-up. Faced then with certain impeachment and probable conviction, Nixon resigned the presidency on August 8, 1974. In assuming the office of chief executive, Vice-President Gerald R. Ford declared that "our long national nightmare is at last over." Ford subsequently pardoned Nixon, a highly controversial act that nonetheless brought the affair to its final conclusion.

On May 9, 1974, the House Judiciary Committee, chaired by Peter Rodino of New Jersey, began its inquiry into the possible impeachment of President Nixon.

On August 9, 1974—his last morning as president of the United States—an emotional Richard Nixon bid farewell to members of his cabinet and White House staff.

# THE WHOLE WORLD IS WATCHING

## The Trial of the Chicago Seven

*Quite often, highly publicized trials become circus-like spectacles in which the antics outside the courtroom overshadow the legal proceedings themselves. The celebrated 1969/70 trial of the Chicago Seven, however, needed no media hype to turn it into an event. It was an exercise in pure theater, produced by the defendants to dramatize what they considered to be the trial's absurdity. Zany though they were, the proceedings nonetheless exposed an intolerant local political machine which had systematically attempted to deny a huge coalition of liberal organizations its right to demonstrate against the war in Southeast Asia.*

*In August 1969, as the Democratic National Convention prepared to open in Chicago, groups opposing U.S. involvement in South Vietnam began congregating in the Windy City to protest the war. They included the National Mobilization Committee to End the War in Vietnam (MOBE), Students for a Democratic Society (SDS), and the Youth International Party (the "Yippies"), an organization using absurdist tactics. Groups with grievances other than the war, like the Black Panthers,*

The Chicago Seven meet with the press on October 8, 1969, during the course of their trial for conspiracy to riot. Seated is "Yippi" Jerry Rubin and a friend. Behind him (left to right) are another Yippi, Abbie Hoffman, teachers John Froines and Lee Weiner, David Dellinger of MOBE, and Rennie Davis and Tom Hayden of SDS.

*were also in attendance.*

*Municipal officials, headed by Mayor Richard J. Daley, refused to have their city disrupted. A clash between the police and the demonstrators was inevitable, and it came outside the Hilton Hotel on August 29, 1968, in front of a national TV audience. In the bloody aftermath of the riot, eight demonstrators were brought to trial: Jerry Rubin and*

*Abbie Hoffman of the Yippies, Rennie Davis and Tom Hayden of SDS, David Dellinger of MOBE, teachers John Froines and Lee Weiner, and Bobby Seale of the Black Panthers. The charge was conspiracy to riot.*

*The trial, which began on September 26, 1969, lasted almost five months, with 74-year-old Judge Julius Hoffman presiding. On day one, Seale* demanded a separate trial while accusing the judge of racism. Although the defendant's repeated outbursts led Hoffman to have him bound and gagged, Seale was finally granted his request. Minus Seale, the remaining defendants became the celebrated Chicago Seven.

The trial became so bizarre that it could have been played out to the tune of a slide whistle! When the judge prohibited flamboyant defense attorneys William Kunstler and Leonard Weinglass from calling U.S. Attorney General Ramsey Clark as a witness, they decided to expose through humor what they felt was a mockery of justice, calling instead on a long list of celebrity witnesses, including Norman Mailer, Julian Bond, and Dick Gregory, and allowing them to testify about anything they wished. Even beat poet Allen Ginsberg took the stand and chanted the Hare Krishna mantra. Other displays of playful indignation included draping the defense table with U.S. and North Vietnamese flags and garbing the defendants in judicial robes.

But when the trial came to an end on February 15, 1970, the Chicago Seven were acquitted of conspiracy to riot, although five of the group were convicted of a lesser charge, crossing state lines to incite riot. Moreover, their boisterous antics during the trial netted them sentences for contempt of court. But, in the final act of the comic melodrama, their convictions were overturned by a federal district judge. Hoffman had waited too long to impose the sentences.

Defense attorney William Kunstler tells a Chicago policeman that he is carrying his records in a box marked "Stuff for the Defense Trial."

Presiding over the conspiracy trial was 74-year-old U.S. District Court Judge Julius Hoffman.

# MISCARRIAGE OF JUSTICE

## The Sacco and Vanzetti Case

Bartolomeo Vanzetti (left) and Nicola Sacco, seen here during their trial, were convicted of murder and robbery. Their real crimes, however, were simply being immigrants and anarchists.

*F*ollowing Russia's Bolshevik Revolution in 1917, the world reacted with shock and fear to the great unknown—Communism. Compounded by the horrors of World War I and the mass migration of immigrants over the preceding decades, the United States in particular sought to protect itself against the Red menace, enacting strict legislation against un-American sentiment—notably the Alien and Sedition Acts of 1918—and coming down hard on those who did not comply. In 1921, Nicola Sacco and Bartolomeo Vanzetti were among the first to feel the impact of this new conservatism.

The two anarchists were among the wave of Italians who immigrated to the United States early in the 20th century. In 1917, the year the United States entered the war, they fled to Mexico to avoid the draft, but returned shortly thereafter. Settling in eastern Massachusetts, Sacco became a shoemaker and Vanzetti a fish peddler. On April 15, 1920, in the small town of South Braintree, Massachusetts, two shoe factory employees,

This Massachusetts courthouse was the scene of the trial in 1921. Six years of appeals and inquiries followed, however, before the defendants were put to death in August 1927.

Frederick A. Parmenter and Alessandro Beradelli, were found murdered and a payroll of more than $15,000 disappeared. Less than a month later, the police arrested Sacco and Vanzetti for the crimes. According to the arresting officers, the immigrants had been carrying guns and had behaved suspiciously during their interrogation. They were charged not only with the shoe factory murder, but also with an unrelated holdup.

The ensuing trial was played out in a climate of fear and anger, as the press, which focused on Sacco and Vanzetti's political beliefs as well as their blue-collar and immigrant status, further polarized the rift between aliens and native-born Americans, and between unionists and those who were promanagement. Despite the largely circumstantial evidence against them, Sacco and Vanzetti were found guilty of first-degree murder on July 14, 1921, and sentenced to die in the electric chair.

For the next six years, Sacco and Vanzetti engaged in a lengthy appeals process, as

Following the convictions of Sacco
and Vanzetti, protest marches and
labor strikes were held around the
globe. Even noted celebrities such
as H. G. Wells and Albert Einstein
lent their support to the anarchists.

protest marches and labor strikes were held around the globe on their behalf. Noted celebrities such as H. G. Wells, Edna St. Vincent Millay, Upton Sinclair, and Albert Einstein lent their support to the anarchists, while legal scholar Felix Frankfurter examined the flaws of the case against them in Atlantic Monthly, pointing out the apparent bias of the presiding judge, Webster Thayer. Even the FBI got involved, investigating Thayer, as well as Governor Alvan T. Fuller of Massachusetts.

Despite the support they received, Sacco and Vanzetti were executed on August 23, 1927. Following their deaths, thousands mourned in a Boston funeral procession that stretched for eight miles.

Although many considered their deaths unconscionable miscarriages of justice, Sacco and Vanzetti themselves felt that they went to the electric chair as martyrs in a worthwhile cause. As Vanzetti put it after his conviction, "If it had not been for these thing, I might have lived out my life talking at street corners to scorning men. I might have died unmarked, unknown, a failure. . . . [But now] that last moment belongs to us—that agony is our triumph."

Mourners file past the open coffins of Sacco and Vanzetti. This scene inspired a painting by artist Ben Shahn, now in the Whitney Museum of American Art in New York.

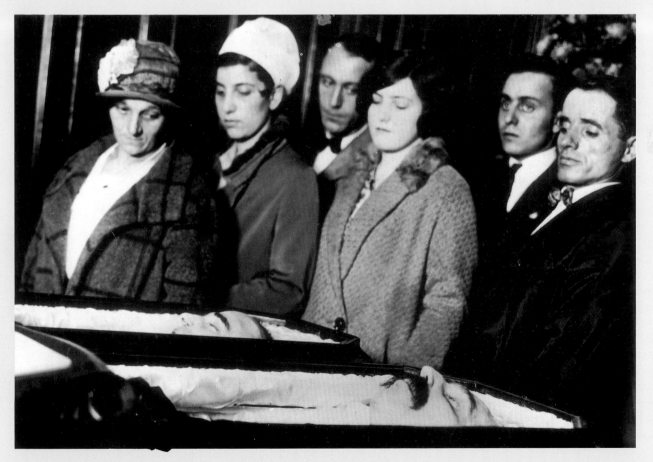

*Until the early 1970s, women in Texas were denied the right to have legal abortions because of a statute that was enacted by the state legislature before the Civil War. As a consequence, thousands of women resorted in desperation to "back alley" procedures under conditions best described as unsanitary and deplorable. Then in 1973 the U.S. Supreme Court took a stand on the issue of abortion, ensuring the right of choice not only to women in Texas but also to those across the nation. The case in which this landmark decision was made is known as Roe v. Wade.*

*Jane Roe (pseudonym for Norma McCorvey) was a single woman working in Dallas who wanted to terminate her pregnancy. She tried to get an abortion, and then discovered that the procedure was forbidden by Texas law. Questioning the efficacy of the statute, she consulted attorney Sarah Weddington and others who were waiting for just such a test case. Agreeing to serve as the trailblazer for millions of other women, McCorvey filed suit in 1970 in federal court against district attorney Henry Wade in order to prevent him from enforcing the law.*

*Although it held in favor of Roe, the three-judge federal court didn't take a position with regard to the statute. The case was then referred to the U.S. Supreme Court.*

*On January 22, 1973, the high court issued its opinion, which declared the state law*

A smiling Norma McCorvey (left)—"Jane Roe"—and attorney Gloria Allred leave the Supreme Court, scene of their 1973 triumph, after presenting oral arguments in the 1989 case of *Webster v. Reproductive Health Services.* They lost that battle, however.

# THE RIGHT TO CHOICE

## Roe v. Wade

On January 22, 1973, the Supreme Court declared unconstitutional state statutes prohibiting abortions during a woman's first trimester. On the bench at the time were (left to right, front row) Stewart, Douglas, Burger, Brennan, and White; (back row) Powell, Marshall, Blackman, and Rehnquist (who dissented along with White).

The daughter of a west Texas preacher, attorney Sarah Weddington presented the case for the plaintiff in *Roe v. Wade* before the U.S. Supreme Court. She later became a senior adviser to President Jimmy Carter.

unconstitutional. For the first time in the history of the United States, a state's abortion statutes had been deemed to violate fundamental civil liberties guaranteed in the Bill of Rights, marking the beginning of the end of such laws across the nation.

In the years since this controversial decision, antiabortion advocates and legislators have continued to make their opinions known, and have looked for opportuni-ties to overturn the decision. The late 1980s saw a change in the basic character of the Supreme Court, as more liberal justices were replaced by conservative appointees of President Ronald Reagan, and this change has clearly given right-to-life advocates renewed hope. And indeed indications of possible change in the court's position on the issue can be seen in the 1989 case of Webster v. Reproductive Health Services. While the court's ruling in this instance didn't overturn Roe v. Wade, it gave states more autonomy over their statutes by ruling that public funds and employees could be withheld from abortion cases. Exactly where the high court is headed regarding this heated issue remains uncer-tain, but undoubtedly the controversy over the right of choice in pregnancies will continue to engender wide-spread debate.

# A "FIFTH" A DAY

## The Kefauver Hearings

On May 18, 1950, the work of the Special Committee to Investigate Crime in Interstate Commerce began, as its chairman, Sen. Estes Kefauver (right), met with committee members Charles Tobey of New Hampshire and Alexander Wiley of Wisconsin and chief counsel Rudolph Halley.

*The soft-spoken senator from Tennessee adjusted his glasses and repeated his question to Jake "Greasy Thumb" Guzik. Had Guzik been involved in the murder of a gambling associate? With inadvertent humor, the evasive mobster refused to reply on the grounds that "My answers might discriminate against me." Such were the responses that Estes Kefauver frequently received during the two years that he questioned hundreds of underworld figures*

*in what became known as the Kefauver hearings.*

*The Senate Special Committee to Investigate Crime in Interstate Commerce sprang from Kefauver's belief in an organized crime syndicate operating in the United States, an organization then almost entirely unknown to the American public. Hoping that he could generate widespread awareness of the mob's pervasive influence in business and government, the senator*

*launched his investigation. Other committee members included Lester Hunt of Wyoming, Herbert R. O'Connor of Maryland, Charles W. Tobey of New Hampshire, and Alexander Wiley of Wisconsin.*

*The hearings opened in May 1950 behind closed doors but within a month they went public as the committee members toured the country, interviewing witnesses in such cities as Miami, Los Angeles, New York, Chicago, and New*

Orleans. In January 1951, television began to carry the sessions, attracting an immense viewing audience of between 20 and 30 million. Through the testimony of hundreds of mob-connected figures, the public saw a grim story unfold.

Many of the gangsters who came before the committee weren't exactly volunteers. Some, like Al Capone's lieutenant Anthony J."Joe Batters" Accardo, repeatedly refused to answer questions by taking the Fifth Amendment. Acknowledged mob leader Frank Costello even lost his temper on the witness stand and stalked out of the hearings. But, not wishing to incur a contempt citation, he returned. Despite its difficulty with witnesses, the committee saw some positive results. Gangsters like Joseph "Joe Adonis" Doto were jailed and/or fined. Some were even deported.

In September 1951, after hearing almost 800 witnesses, the committee brought its investigation to an end. Its four concluding reports confirmed that an organized criminal network indeed operated on an expansive scale throughout the United States. The hearings woke people up to the menace in their midst. And they made Estes Kefauver a national figure. The tall, lanky senator ran for president a year later and became the Democratic party's vice-presidential nominee in 1956.

Longshoreman Joseph Anastasia, brother of notorious mobster Albert Anastasia, awaits deportation at the hands of the U.S. Immigration and Naturalization Service in 1951 as a result of information obtained by the Kefauver committee.

## Photo Credits

Silhouetted in the shadow of the U.S. capitol building is the youngest attorney general in American history, Robert Francis Kennedy.